BELIEVE YOUR OWN MIND

NARC-PROOFING YOUR KIDS WHEN YOU CO-PARENT WITH A BORDERLINE, NARCISSISTIC, OR TOXIC EX

AYO BOMANI

First edition November 2024
ISBN 978-2-3167-6319-0 (eBook)
Published by Success Publications
www.believeyourownmind.com

DEDICATION

To those navigating the challenges of co-parenting
with a toxic ex, and to my kids, who have been my constant
motivation. This book represents our journey
and the determination to find peace
and strength amidst the difficulties.

CONTENTS

SOME IMPORTANT NOTES

Disclaimer

This book is not a legal guide, nor is it a substitute for professional mental health care, psychological diagnosis, or therapy. The information provided within these pages is intended for educational and informational purposes only. Your attorney, doctor, or therapist are the best resources for legal advice, medical treatment, or mental health support tailored to your specific circumstances.

Please use your best judgment when considering the advice and recommendations presented in this guide. Every situation is unique, and what may work for one individual or family may not be suitable for another. It is important to carefully consider the information provided and consult with appropriate professionals before making any significant decisions or taking action.

If you ever feel that your or your child's life is in danger, do not hesitate to seek immediate assistance from your local police department or emergency services. Your safety and well-being are paramount, and it is crucial to prioritize your physical and emotional health in times of crisis.

Affiliate Links Disclosure

The eBook version of this book contains affiliate links, which means that the author may earn a commission from qualifying purchases made through these links. This helps to support the author's work and allows them to continue providing valuable content to readers. Rest assured that all affiliate links are carefully selected and recommended based on their relevance and usefulness to the content of this book. Your support is greatly appreciated.

Affiliation

The author is not affiliated with any brands mentioned in this book other than Believe Your Own Mind. Any references to specific products or services are for informational purposes only and do not constitute endorsements.

HELPFUL RESOURCES

In addition to this book, check out these resources to help keep you on track and well-supported as you make changes in your life:

- Add to your network of supportive people who understand what you're going through by joining the Believe Your Own Mind community.

- Learn more about narc-proofing your children by taking the Protecting Your Child's Mental Health in a High-Conflict Co-Parenting Situation course.

- Let the Believe Your Own Mind app be your daily cheerleader— add the Believe Your Own Mind app to your network of support.

- Sign up for the Believe Your Own Mind newsletter to stay up-to-date with the latest developments.

HOW TO USE THIS BOOK

Welcome to Believe Your Own Mind! This guide is designed to provide practical strategies, insights, and resources to support you in navigating the challenges of co-parenting with a toxic co-parent while prioritizing the well-being of your child. Here's how to make the most of this resource:

1. **Not all suggestions in this book will resonate with you, and that's okay.** Firstly, this book assumes you are not cohabitating with your co-parent. In addition, each family dynamic is unique, and what works for one may not work for another. Feel free to pick and choose the strategies and recommendations that best suit your situation and align with your values.

2. **Action Items for Your Consideration:** These sections within some chapters present actionable steps you can take to implement the concepts discussed. Browse through the list and choose the action items that resonate most with you and your family. This section also provides a curated list of books, websites, videos, social media accounts, and other resources to support you in applying the action items outlined in the chapter. Explore these resources to gain further insights and guidance on your journey.

By engaging with the content, reflecting on the action items, and utilizing the recommended resources, you can empower yourself to navigate co-parenting challenges with confidence and resilience.

Let's embark on this journey together, prioritizing the well-being of our children and fostering a legacy of love, strength, and resilience in our families.

I hope the pages of this book bring you hope for the future of your children and the life you are about to create!

Ayo Bomani

PREFACE
A WORD ON REALITY

Some people will try to feed you a diet of their warped reality. When you notice patterns that reveal their reality isn't reliable or that they're distorting the truth to pull you into the cult of their disturbed thinking, do not consume what they're serving.

It's junk food.

It's bad for you. It's bad for your children.

Trust yourself.

Believe your own mind.

CHAPTER 1
WHO I AM

My relationship with my co-parent left me grappling with confusion, struggling to discern my own reality, and coping with the aftermath of severe emotional trauma.

In the grand scheme of things, my personal story pales in comparison to the journey you're embarking on as you navigate co-parenting with a toxic co-parent. However, I believe it's important to provide some context, so here's a brief glimpse into my own experience.

My journey with co-parenting began with a husband who exhibited erratic behavior, volatility, and covert narcissistic traits throughout our near-decade-long marriage. While his therapist once suggested he might have borderline personality disorder, I've learned that labels matter less than the impact of the behaviors themselves. Regardless of the diagnostic label, my relationship with him left me grappling with confusion, struggling to discern my own reality, and coping with the aftermath of severe emotional trauma.

After our marriage ended, he deployed his volatile, erratic, and abusive behavior on our young children to the extent that mediation, attorney-involvement, and several investigations by Child Protective Services were required. I've used the strategies outlined in this book to remedy my ex's counter-parenting and the harm he attempts to cause to our children.

Armed with an educational background including a master's in education from the University of Southern California, I've dedicated myself to understanding and navigating the complexities of co-parenting in the face of adversity. However, due to the potential for legal repercussions from my ex-husband with whom I am still co-parenting, I've chosen to use a pseudonym to write this book.

But enough about me. Let's focus on what truly matters: your journey, your challenges, and your triumphs as you strive to create a safe and nurturing environment for your children amidst the complexities of co-parenting with a toxic co-parent.

I want to assure you that every strategy, insight, and recommendation presented in this book is rooted in my own experiences and practices with my young children. Despite the trials and tribulations, my kids are thriving, happy, and healthy—a testament to the resilience of the human spirit and the power of intentional parenting.

As we embark on this journey together, my hope is that the lessons learned and shared within these pages will empower you to navigate the twists and turns of co-parenting with courage, grace, and unwavering determination. Your children deserve nothing less, and I believe that with the right tools and support, you can build a bright and hopeful future for them—one filled with love, resilience, and boundless possibilities.

So, let's dive in and explore the strategies, insights, and resources that will guide you on this transformative journey toward creating a legacy of wellness and resilience for your family.

With warmest regards,

Ayo Bomani

CHAPTER 2

WHO BENEFITS FROM THIS BOOK: BUILDING A LEGACY OF WELLNESS

I don't want my children to end up in the kinds of relationships I have been in.

If you're reading this, you might be navigating the treacherous waters of co-parenting with a toxic individual, or perhaps you're concerned about safeguarding your children from falling prey to toxic personalities like those with borderline personality disorder (BPD), narcissistic personality disorder (NPD), sociopathy, or other related conditions. Maybe you're like me, someone who has been through unhealthy relationships and is determined to break the cycle for the sake of your children. Whatever your reason for picking up this book, know that you're not alone, and there is hope for a brighter future.

I often say that I don't want my children to end up in the kinds of relationships I have been in. This sentiment might resonate deeply with you. As parents and guardians, we have a profound responsibility to nurture and protect the next generation from the harmful patterns and behaviors that we've experienced firsthand. It's not just about shielding them from immediate harm but equipping them with the tools and knowledge to thrive in healthy relationships throughout their lives.

The journey towards creating a legacy of wellness begins with acknowledging that this book is not about the toxic or narcissistic person. It's about you and the profound impact you can have on shaping a positive future for your children and their descendants. While it's natural to be consumed by the chaos and toxicity of co-parenting with someone who exhibits destructive behaviors, this book is a reminder that you hold the power to cultivate an environment of safety, stability, and love for your children.

Throughout these pages, you'll find a myriad of suggestions, strategies, and insights tailored to support you on your journey. From practical tips for managing co-parenting dynamics with a toxic individual to guidance on fostering resilience and emotional intelligence in your children, each chapter is designed to empower you with the knowledge and resources needed to navigate these challenging circumstances.

But here's the most important thing I want to share with you: this book is about the legacy of wellness you're giving your child and your descendants. It's about breaking free from the cycles of dysfunction and creating a ripple effect of healing that extends far beyond your immediate family. By investing in your own well-being and actively working to create a healthy environment for your children, you're laying the foundation for a brighter and more harmonious future for generations to come.

As you delve into the chapters ahead, keep in mind that not all suggestions will resonate with you, and that's okay. Every family dynamic is unique, and what works for one may not work for another. Take what aligns with your values and circumstances and leave behind what doesn't. Trust your instincts as a parent and know that you are capable of guiding your family towards a future filled with love, resilience, and abundance.

Whether it's books, websites, support groups, or therapeutic services, there is a wealth of support available to you as you embark on this journey of healing and transformation. You are not alone, and together, we can build a legacy of wellness that transcends the confines of toxic relationships and paves the way for a brighter tomorrow.

CHAPTER 3

WHO YOU ARE: NURTURING YOUR FAMILY'S VISION

This book will help you stand firm in your truth, **believe your own mind***, and protect your child from the confusion your co-parent is trying to create.*

More important than who I am is who you are. You are someone who embodies qualities that lay the groundwork for a thriving family dynamic. You possess firm boundaries, a clear vision for your family's future, and unwavering confidence in your parenting decisions. You understand the importance of allowing your parenting style to evolve for the better, rejecting harmful practices such as name-calling or physical discipline, and embracing consistency as a cornerstone of your family's fabric.

You recognize that modeling good values and behavior is paramount, and while you strive for excellence, you understand that perfection is not the goal. Anything implemented consistently, no matter how small, contributes to the well-being and protection of your child. You are committed to your own growth and well-being, understanding that only by being healthy and balanced yourself can you effectively model what health, well-being, and good boundaries look like for your children.

It may feel daunting to bridge the gap between where you are now and the ideal scenario outlined above. Perhaps you're grappling with symptoms of PTSD stemming from emotional or physical abuse—confusion, disillusionment, fear, anxiety, guilt, shame, low self-esteem, and low self-confidence. I vividly recall describing to a therapist the overwhelming sense of confusion that plagued me in the aftermath of my separation.

But here's what I want you to know: you, your children, and your children's children are worth every ounce of effort it takes to safeguard their mental, emotional, and physical well-being while navigating the complexities of co-parenting with a toxic individual.

To get from where you are now to where you want to be, you must keep your mind right and not get caught up in the delusions and alternate narratives your toxic co-parent creates. Their relentless attempts to gaslight, manipulate, and control are designed to make you question your reality, infecting your thoughts like a brainworm. But this book will help you stand firm in your truth, **believe your own mind**, and protect your child from the confusion your co-parent is trying to create. No matter how persistent their efforts to make you doubt yourself, you will find the strength here to hold onto your reality, stay grounded for your child, and remain unshaken.

Hold firm to your boundaries, even when they're tested. Hold fast to your vision for your children's future, even when the path seems uncertain. Stay resilient in the face of adversity, drawing strength from the knowledge that your unwavering commitment to your family's well-being will shape generations to come.

Above all, trust in your own intuition and judgment. Your instincts as a parent are a powerful compass, guiding you towards the best decisions for your family. Stay true to yourself, stay grounded in your values, and never doubt the strength and resilience within you.

As you embark on this journey of nurturing your family's vision, know that you are not alone. Together, we can create a future where love, respect, and compassion prevail, breaking free from the chains of toxicity and laying the foundation for a legacy of wellness that spans generations.

☐ Install and use the Mama Zen app.

☐ Install and use the Believe Your Own Mind app.

☐ Install and use the Bloom app.

☐ Install and use I Am affirmations app.

☐ See a therapist through BetterHelp or Talkspace.

☐ See an in-person therapist,

☐ Read parenting books.

☐ Read child development books.

☐ Read Codependent No More.

☐ Educate yourself on Cluster B Personality Disorders.

☐ Attend Codependents Anonymous meetings.

☐ Join online groups for survivors of narcissistic abuse.

CHAPTER 4
YOU ARE NOT CRAZY

I want to reiterate an important point: you've arrived here for a good reason. You're not imagining danger, and you're certainly not overreacting when you express concern about your child's well-being in the hands of their other parent. It's vital to acknowledge that the subtle attacks you perceive, which may only become evident after observing a pattern of behavior over time, are indeed real and dangerous. Just because the threat is often invisible or hard to identify doesn't make it any less significant.

Many people might look at your situation and dismiss it as paranoia, but you know the truth. You've witnessed the chaos mixed with moments of apparent decency, making it all the more confusing to decipher the true nature of the other parent. This inconsistency can lead others to believe that you're dealing with a reasonable individual, but deep down, you understand that's not the case.

The ability to see through the façade and recognize the underlying patterns of dysfunctional behavior is what has brought you here. You are not crazy; you are observant, and you are aware of the dynamics at play. This knowledge is crucial for your own peace of mind and for the safety of your children. Just because others may not see the dangers at first glance doesn't mean they don't exist. You are living in a reality that many may not understand, but that doesn't diminish its validity.

It's critical you believe in your own mind and trust your instincts. The doubts that the other parent may throw your way are merely attempts to undermine your perception of reality. You know what you're dealing with, and that clarity will serve as your compass as you navigate this tumultuous journey. Your ability to recognize the truth is one of the most powerful tools you possess as a parent.

What you find within these pages is not just advice, it is some of the most important work you will do for yourself and your children. The guidance here is centered on instituting and cultivating protective factors to guard against Adverse Childhood Experiences (ACEs). You are not delusional, but even if we briefly entertain the notion for argument's sake, the advice provided here is beneficial for the mental health and emotional well-being of your child.

By following these principles, you will equip your child with the skills to spot tricky people and protect themselves from manipulation and harm. You are teaching them resilience, emotional intelligence, and self-advocacy. These are invaluable lessons that will serve them throughout their lives, helping them navigate not only their current situation but any challenges they may face in the future.

Always remember that you are not crazy. You are strong, capable, and aware of the truth. Your journey begins with believing in yourself, trusting your instincts, and understanding that you are doing the essential work of safeguarding your child's future.

CHAPTER 5

WHAT YOU'RE UP AGAINST: NAVIGATING CO-PARENTING WITH A NARCISSISTIC PARTNER

The abuse from a narcissistic co-parent can take various forms, each with its own detrimental effects on both you and your children.

Having co-parented with a narcissist, I understand firsthand the challenges and complexities that come with navigating such a relationship, especially when children are involved. Whether you're currently in the throes of coping with a narcissistic co-parent or preparing to navigate such a relationship, it's essential to recognize the potential impact that your partner's behavior can have on your children's well-being.

My most recent experience was with a partner who exhibited covert narcissistic traits, which manifested in subtle psychological manipulation and abuse. However, I've also had the unfortunate experience of dealing with a malignant or obvious narcissist who was not only psychologically abusive but also physically violent.

The abuse from a narcissistic co-parent can take various forms, each with its own detrimental effects on both you and your children. One common tactic is the silent treatment, used to manipulate and control the other person into complying with their wishes. This form of emotional manipulation can leave the victim feeling isolated, anxious, and powerless, while also setting a harmful example for the children about how to resolve conflicts in relationships.

Another insidious behavior to watch out for is sabotage, revenge, or counter-parenting—actions taken by the narcissistic co-parent to undermine your authority or disrupt the well-being of your children. Whether it's intentionally neglecting their responsibilities, undermining your parenting decisions, or seeking revenge for perceived slights, these actions can create a toxic environment for both you and your children, perpetuating a cycle of dysfunction and emotional harm.

It's important to recognize that while you may be able to escape the direct impact of these behaviors when you're not with your co-parent, your children are left vulnerable to their influence every time they're in their care. This realization can be overwhelming and heartbreaking, but it also highlights the urgency of taking proactive steps to protect and support your children as they navigate these challenging dynamics.

In today's digital age, another concern is the co-parent's reliance on technology—such as smartphones—as a means of escaping from their responsibilities and emotionally engaging with their children. This disconnection can further exacerbate feelings of abandonment and neglect in the children as they witness their co-parent prioritizing their own needs and desires over their parental duties.

By prioritizing the needs of your children and advocating for their safety and well-being, you can help mitigate the impact of narcissistic co-parenting and create a more stable and nurturing environment for your family. Your children's future depends on it.

CHAPTER 6

WHY THIS MATTERS: PROTECTING YOUR CHILD'S MIND FROM NARCISSISTIC ABUSE

Narcissistic abuse, whether emotional, psychological, or physical, is a significant ACE that can shape the trajectory of a child's life.

Protecting your child's mind from the potential lifelong effects of narcissistic abuse is one of the most important challenges in life. As you navigate the complexities of co-parenting with a toxic individual, it's crucial to understand the profound impact that narcissistic abuse can have on your child's mental and emotional well-being.

Adverse Childhood Events (ACEs) are traumatic experiences that occur during childhood and can have long-lasting effects on a person's health and well-being. Narcissistic abuse, whether emotional, psychological, or physical, is a significant ACE that can shape the trajectory of a child's life. From chronic stress and anxiety to depression and low self-esteem, the consequences can manifest in a variety of ways, often continuing into adulthood.

Defining ACEs

Adverse Childhood Experiences (ACEs) are tough or traumatic events that kids might experience before the age of 18. These experiences include things like:

- abuse (physical, emotional, or sexual),

- neglect,

- a parent's substance abuse,

- mental health problems in the family,

- domestic violence,

- a family member going to jail,

- or parents getting divorced.

ACEs can really impact a child's health, emotions, and thoughts, and are associated with:

- chronic health issues,

- mental health disorders,

- and substance misuse during adolescence and adulthood,

- and can also have adverse effects on education, career prospects, and income potential.

The consequences of ACEs can impact generations of families, communities, and society. The good news is that ACEs can be prevented.

Mitigating ACEs can lead to the well-being of children and adults, and potential benefits such as:

1. Decreased likelihood of developing conditions such as depression, asthma, cancer, and diabetes in later life.

2. Minimized engagement in addictive behaviors such as smoking and excessive alcohol consumption.

3. Enhanced prospects for education and employment.

4. Breaking the cycle of ACEs being perpetuated from one generation to the next.

ACEs Caused by a Toxic Co-Parent

A narcissistic or toxic parent can create trauma for a child through various behaviors and actions that fall under ACEs. These experiences can have profound and long-lasting effects on a child's life well into adulthood.

1. **Emotional Abuse:** A narcissistic parent may engage in emotional abuse by constantly criticizing, belittling, or invalidating the child's feelings and experiences. This can lead to low self-esteem, feelings of worthlessness, and a distorted self-image in the child. As adults, they may struggle with self-confidence, relationships, and mental health issues.

2. **Manipulation and Gaslighting:** Narcissistic parents often manipulate and gaslight their children, making them doubt their reality, emotions, and perceptions. This can create confusion, anxiety, and a sense of instability in the child's life. As adults, they may struggle with trust issues, difficulty asserting boundaries, and challenges in maintaining healthy relationships.

3. **Neglect:** Narcissistic parents may neglect their child's emotional, physical, and psychological needs, focusing instead on their own desires and agenda. This can result in feelings of abandonment, loneliness, and emotional detachment in the child. As adults, they may struggle with self-care, intimacy, and forming meaningful connections with others.

4. **Control and Overprotection:** Narcissistic parents often exert control and overprotection over their children, limiting their autonomy, independence, and self-expression. This can stifle the child's growth, creativity, and sense of agency. As adults, they may struggle with decision-making, assertiveness, and taking risks in life.

5. **Intermittent Reinforcement:** Narcissistic parents may use intermittent reinforcement, alternating between praise and criticism, love and rejection, to manipulate their child's behavior and emotions. This can create a sense of unpredictability and insecurity in the child's life. As adults, they may struggle with fear of abandonment, difficulty trusting others, and emotional regulation challenges.

These traumatic experiences during childhood can have lasting effects on a child's development, mental health, and well-being into adulthood. They may manifest as symptoms of post-traumatic stress disorder (PTSD), anxiety disorders, depression, low self-esteem, difficulty forming and maintaining relationships, and patterns of self-sabotage or self-destructive behavior.

One of the insidious aspects of narcissistic abuse is the normalization of dysfunction. Children who grow up in environments where abuse is prevalent may come to view such behavior as normal or acceptable, perpetuating a cycle of dysfunction in their own relationships later in life. It's essential to recognize and disrupt this pattern, offering your child a different narrative and model of healthy relationships.

Protective factors play a crucial role in mitigating the impact of narcissistic abuse on children. A supportive and nurturing environment, consistent and loving caregivers, and access to mental health resources can all help buffer the effects of trauma and foster resilience in children. By providing a safe and stable home environment, you can counteract the negative influences of narcissistic co-parenting and empower your child to thrive despite the challenges they may face.

Unfortunately, children who grow up in environments characterized by narcissistic abuse are at a higher likelihood of ending up in similar relationships themselves. Toxic individuals groom others to accept abuse, manipulating and gaslighting their victims into believing that they deserve mistreatment. It's crucial to break this cycle by teaching your child to recognize unhealthy relationship dynamics and empowering them to advocate for their own well-being.

Both emotional and physical abuse can have profound and adverse effects on a child's development. From impaired cognitive function to increased risk of substance abuse and mental health disorders, the consequences of narcissistic abuse can be far-reaching and long-lasting. As a parent, it's your responsibility to shield your child from harm and provide them with the tools and support they need to heal and thrive.

In conclusion, protecting your child's mind from the impact of narcissistic abuse is a monumental task, but one that is essential for their long-term well-being and happiness. By understanding the adverse effects of narcissistic abuse, fostering protective factors, and breaking the cycle of dysfunction, you can empower your child to overcome the challenges they face and build a brighter future free from the shadow of abuse.

CHAPTER 7

CREATING A HAPPY HOME FOR YOUR CHILDREN THROUGH PROTECTIVE FACTORS

Create a home environment where your children can thrive, regardless of the challenges they face outside its walls.

When you think of the word "home," what are some words and images that come to mind? For many of us, the word "home" conjures up feelings of safety, warmth, nostalgia, and belonging. It's a sanctuary where we find comfort and love, a place where we can truly be ourselves. As parents, especially those navigating the complexities of co-parenting, creating a home that embodies these feelings is essential for our children's well-being.

This book is about more than just building a physical space; it's about crafting an environment that is inviting to your children and one that is filled with protective factors, which we'll cover in a moment. A home that feels safe and nurturing allows your kids to flourish emotionally, mentally, and socially. It becomes a model of healthy living, teaching them what a positive, loving environment looks like, and protects them from those who cause them harm.

Protective Factors

Protective factors are the positive influences and conditions that help shield individuals, particularly children, from the potential negative effects of adverse experiences, such as trauma or toxic relationships. These factors include strong friends and family support, healthy relationships, positive self-esteem, and access to resources such as education and mental health services. By fostering protective factors, we can enhance resilience, promote emotional well-being, and empower children to navigate challenges more effectively, ultimately contributing to their long-term success and happiness in life. The ideas in this book are all about being intentional and consistent in deploying protective factors and creating a safe home to protect your children from the long-term traumatic effects of Adverse Childhood Events caused by a dysfunctional co-parent.

The Foundation of Safety and Warmth

To start, we'll dive into what safety and warmth mean in the context of your home. It can be as simple as creating a cozy space for family gatherings, where laughter fills the air and love is palpable. It might involve ensuring that your home is a haven for open conversations, where your children feel secure enough to express their thoughts and feelings without fear of judgment.

Safety can also be about establishing routines that provide stability in their lives. Consistent mealtimes, regular family activities, and bedtime rituals can help create a sense of predictability that allows children to feel grounded. These routines signal to your children that they can rely on you and your home as a secure base, no matter the chaos they may experience outside.

Safety and warmth offer protective factors, and, later in this book, we'll cover a few different ideas on how to create a warm and safe home.

Crafting Beautiful Memories

Nostalgia is a powerful force, especially in childhood. The memories you create in your home will shape your children's perceptions of what "home" means to them as they grow. Think about the experiences you want to foster—family movie nights, baking cookies together, or weekend adventures in nature. Each moment spent together builds a tapestry of beautiful memories that your children will carry with them throughout their lives.

Encourage your children to contribute to the creation of these memories. By involving them, you instill a sense of ownership and pride in their environment, making it even more inviting. This book will cover some ideas for you to consider.

A Model of Healthy Living

Creating a happy home also means modeling healthy habits and relationships. Your home should be a place where respect, kindness, and understanding are at the forefront. Demonstrate healthy communication with your children and model conflict resolution skills. Teach them the importance of self-care, empathy, and support— lessons that will serve them well throughout their lives.

A key aspect of this model is also recognizing the importance of emotional safety. Allow your children to feel and express their emotions freely. Provide a safe space for them to talk about their fears, joys, and frustrations. This emotional validation is crucial for their development and helps them understand that it's okay to experience a wide range of feelings.

Protecting Against Trauma

Finally, a happy home acts as a buffer against trauma. Your role as a parent is to create an environment where they can process these experiences safely. This means listening to their concerns, providing reassurance, and helping them develop coping mechanisms, all of which we'll address in the coming chapters.

Embracing the Vision of Home

This book will help you think of your home as a nurturing haven filled with safety, warmth, and love that can insulate and protect your children from the harms of a parent who perpetuates trauma. As you read this book and take in its suggestions, keep the vision of creating a happy and protective home at the forefront of your mind.

You are crafting more than just a physical space—you are building a legacy of love, resilience, and beautiful memories. This is the essence of a home that protects against trauma and fosters a sense of belonging—an environment where your children can thrive, regardless of the challenges they face outside its walls.

CHAPTER 8
BEING THERE AND BEING YOU: BUILDING MEANINGFUL RELATIONSHIPS THROUGH PRESENCE AND VALUES

In a world that often equates love and affection with material possessions, it's easy to fall into the trap of trying to bribe our children with toys, expensive gifts, or lavish trips. However, as parents navigating the complexities of co-parenting with a toxic individual, it's essential to recognize that true connection and meaningful relationships with our children are not built on superficial gestures or material wealth.

You don't need to compete with the other parent's offerings of toys, gifts, or money. Instead, focus on being a consistent and positive presence in your children's lives. Show them through your actions that your love and support are unwavering, regardless of the material possessions you can provide.

What children truly remember and benefit from the most are the values you instill in them and the quality time you spend together. It's about being a role model of healthy values such as empathy, compassion, integrity, and resilience. These are the qualities that will shape their character and guide them through life's challenges.

Consistency is key. Be there for your children in both the big moments and the small ones. Show up for school events, sports games, and parent-teacher conferences. Listen to their concerns, celebrate their achievements, and offer guidance when they face obstacles. Your presence and support will foster a sense of security and trust that forms the foundation of a strong parent-child relationship.

While the other parent may attempt to buy their affection with material possessions, recognize that these superficial gestures pale in comparison to the depth of emotional connection and understanding that you can cultivate with your children. Rather than trying to outdo them in a materialistic arms race, focus on building an emotionally meaningful relationship based on trust, respect, and genuine connection.

Ultimately, it's the memories of shared experiences, heartfelt conversations, and moments of unconditional love that will leave a lasting impression on your children. These are the building blocks of a relationship that transcends material wealth and stands the test of time.

So, resist the temptation to compete on a shallow level. Instead, invest your time, energy, and resources into nurturing a bond with your children that is grounded in authenticity and mutual respect. Embrace the opportunity to be a positive influence in their lives, guiding them towards a future filled with happiness, fulfillment, and emotional well-being.

In the end, it's not the toys or expensive gifts that matter most—it's the love, support, and presence you provide that make all the difference. Trust in the power of your role as a parent and know that your influence extends far beyond material possessions. By embodying healthy values and consistently showing up for your children, you are laying the groundwork for a relationship that will enrich their lives for years to come.

CHAPTER 9

RETHINKING JOINT CUSTODY: PROTECTING YOUR CHILD'S WELL-BEING IN CO-PARENTING AGREEMENTS

It's time to rethink traditional joint custody arrangements and prioritize the emotional well-being of children in co-parenting agreements.

In the realm of family law and therapy, joint custody arrangements are often touted as the ideal solution for co-parenting following separation or divorce. However, the emphasis on equal parenting time fails to adequately address the nuances of emotional abuse and its profound impact on children's well-being. Unlike physical abuse, emotional abuse leaves no visible scars, making it easier to overlook by those fortunate enough not to have experienced its devastating effects firsthand.

It's time to challenge the assumption that 50/50 custody arrangements are always in the best interest of the child. While the desire for equal time with both parents is understandable, it's essential to consider the quality of parenting each child receives during their time with each parent. Even a small reduction in parenting time for the other parent can provide children with more time in a healthier and nurturing environment—with you.

In crafting co-parenting agreements, work with your attorney and even working with a divorce coach who specializes in high-conflict situations to include provisions that prioritize the emotional well-being of your children. This may include parenting plan provisions like allowing evening calls with the kids while they're at the other parent's house, providing them with a cell phone designed for children's safety and communication like a Gabb phone, mutual agreement to use positive discipline methods only, and mutual agreement to refrain from bad-mouthing the other parent.

Additionally, it's essential to address potential sources of toxic influence within the other parent's network, such as limiting contact with "flying monkeys"—individuals who act as enablers or allies of the toxic parent. Provisions can be added to co-parenting agreements to restrict contact with certain relatives or individuals who may exacerbate the emotional abuse experienced by the children.

Furthermore, it's imperative to acknowledge and address any diagnosed mental health issues that may impact the other parent's ability to provide a safe and nurturing environment for the children. Including language in co-parenting agreements that recognizes and limits parenting time based on the other parent's mental health issues can help to protect the children and ensure they are not exposed to harmful behaviors or environments. For instance, if your co-parent has been diagnosed with borderline personality disorder, or has a documented history of substance abuse, it may be possible to include verbiage in your parenting plan that limits their time with your children owing to the diagnosis. Talk with your attorney about what is possible.

While some may argue that these provisions are difficult to enforce or are unnecessary, being intentional about the protective provisions you include in your parenting plan will lay the groundwork for a stable and nurturing environment in which your children can thrive.

It's time to rethink traditional joint custody arrangements and prioritize the emotional well-being of children in co-parenting agreements. By considering the impact of emotional abuse, implementing additional provisions to safeguard your children, and advocating for their needs, you can create a healthier and more supportive co-parenting dynamic that prioritizes their well-being above all else. Work with your attorney to craft a parenting plan that helps insulate your child from harm.

Action Items for Your Consideration

- ☐ Check Facebook groups for survivors of narcissistic abuse for suggestions—there, you'll find a wealth of real-world experiences.

- ☐ Brainstorm with your family law attorney.

- ☐ Work with a divorce coach or parenting plan coach who specializes in high-conflict situations.

CHAPTER 10

MAKING A HOUSE A HOME: NURTURING YOUR CHILD'S SENSE OF BELONGING

Even the littlest gestures, if done consistently, can make such a huge difference in fostering a sense of belonging and security for your children.

In the hustle and bustle of daily life, it's easy to overlook the profound impact that even the smallest gestures can have on our children's sense of belonging and well-being. Yet, when it comes to raising kids, every little thing matters—from the words we use to the environments we create within our homes.

You'll be surprised by how even the littlest gestures, if done consistently, can make such a huge difference in fostering a sense of belonging and security for your children. As the saying goes, "Not every little thing matters but also every little thing matters." Here are some simple yet impactful ways to nurture your child's sense of belonging:

Let Your Kids Express Themselves: Allow your children to decorate their own rooms or designate a space in your living room for their artwork to be proudly displayed. This not only gives them a sense of ownership over their space but also validates their creativity and individuality.

Our House, Our Home: Consistently refer to your home as "our house" rather than "my house." This subtle change in wording reinforces the idea that the home belongs to the entire family, not just one individual. It fosters a sense of collective ownership and unity among family members.

Prioritize Your Children: Create an environment where your children feel valued and respected. This means prioritizing their needs and interests, whether it's having toys and games they enjoy readily available or stocking up on craft supplies for budding artists. By making their interests a priority, you show them that their presence and contributions are valued in the home.

Foster a Sense of Community: Invite friends and family over frequently to create a sense of community and connection for your children. Sharing meals, playing games, or simply spending time together strengthens familial bonds and provides a supportive network for your children to lean on.

Support Their Passions: Take an active interest in your children's passions and interests. Ask them about their hobbies, notice their achievements, and show support by finding clubs or classes for them to attend. Whether it's joining a sports team, participating in a theater group, or taking art classes, nurturing their interests outside of the home fosters a sense of belonging and fulfillment.

Remember, the little things you do each day—from the words you use to the activities you engage in—shape your child's sense of belonging and identity. By creating a home environment where they feel valued, supported, and loved, you lay the foundation for a lifetime of confidence, resilience, and connection. So, embrace the power of small gestures and watch as they make a big impact on your child's life.

Action Items for Your Consideration

- ☐ Let your kids decorate their room or have a place in your living room for their art to be displayed.

- ☐ Consistently call your house "our house." "This is our home. Not just my home." This simple change of wording matters and encourages your child to feel like they are an integral part of the family.

- ☐ Prioritize your children—not in a way that they are the center of the universe, but so that the home feels like theirs too. For example, have toys and games they enjoy available, always have craft supplies ready for kids interested in crafts, etc.

- ☐ Invite friends and family over frequently (see chapter: A Community of Health).

- ☐ Ask your kids about or notice their passions and interests and nurture them by finding clubs and classes at school or community centers for them to attend. Show support by attending with them.

CHAPTER 11

RUNNING YOUR FAMILY LIKE A BUSINESS: PRIORITIZING PEACE AND HEALTH

Your home should feel like a sanctuary.

In the fast-paced chaos of modern life, it's easy for the needs of the family to get lost along the way. But what if we approached family life with the same intentionality and organization as we do when running a business? By adopting a strategic mindset and prioritizing peace and health as our guiding principles, we can create a home environment that fosters harmony, growth, and well-being for all.

At the heart of running your family like a business is the development of a clear mission and vision statement. Just as a business defines its purpose and goals to guide its actions, so too should a family articulate its core values and aspirations. This mission and vision statement serves as a compass, directing decisions and actions towards the collective well-being of the family unit.

Peace and health are paramount in this endeavor. While perfection is an unrealistic standard, creating a safe and nurturing home environment where everyone feels valued and supported is essential.

Your home should feel like a sanctuary—a place where your children can thrive emotionally, mentally, and physically.

To help keep yourself and your family on track, utilize organizational tools such as planners, calendars, and task lists. By staying organized and proactive, you can minimize stress and maximize productivity, creating space for meaningful connection and quality time with your loved ones.

But running your family like a business isn't just about logistics—it's also about cultivating a shared sense of purpose and vision. Get your children involved by doing a vision board together, where each family member can express their dreams and aspirations for the future. This collaborative exercise fosters communication, creativity, and a sense of unity as you work towards common goals.

Take it a step further by sitting down with your kids, even the littlest ones, to craft your family's mission and vision statement. Discuss what values are important to your family—whether it's kindness, integrity, or resilience—and articulate how you plan to embody these values in your daily lives. This process not only strengthens family bonds but also reinforces the importance of collective responsibility and shared goals.

Finally, don't hesitate to dive deeper into nurturing a family culture that reflects your values and aspirations. Whether it's through books, workshops, or online resources, seek out guidance and inspiration to help cultivate a home environment that promotes growth, connection, and well-being for all.

By running your family like a business with a clear mission and vision, prioritizing peace and health, and utilizing organizational tools and collaborative exercises, you can create a home environment where everyone feels valued, supported, and empowered to thrive. Remember, the journey towards a happy and harmonious family life begins with intentionality, communication, and a shared commitment to peace and health.

Action Items for Your Consideration

- [ ] Create a family calendar on Google Calendar or use your phone calendar and add your family activities and traditions for the next two weeks. If you prefer, buy a physical planner or calendar to keep yourself on track, and remember to add your activities in your planner or calendar.

- [ ] Schedule time to create a vision board with your children. Ask them what goals they'd like your family to accomplish this year and next. You can even ask your children how they'd like to be able to describe their childhood when they are adults.

- [ ] With your kids, write your family's mission and vision statement.

- [ ] Read more about nurturing a family culture: The Book of New Family Traditions: How to Create Great Rituals for Holidays and Every Day.

CHAPTER 12

BUILDING FAMILY TRADITIONS: CREATING LASTING MEMORIES

Rituals and routines play a vital role in shaping family culture and creating lasting memories.

In the tapestry of family life, traditions are the colorful threads that weave together to create a sense of belonging, continuity, and joy. Whether big or small, these rituals and routines play a vital role in shaping family culture and creating lasting memories that will be cherished for years to come. Like an annual company picnic or holiday party, traditions make life fun and pleasant, providing moments of connection and celebration amidst the hustle and bustle of daily life.

When it comes to building family traditions, the possibilities are endless. From holidays and birthdays to vacations and seasonal outings, there are countless opportunities to create meaningful experiences that bring your family closer together. Here are just a few ideas to inspire your own traditions:

Celebrate the holidays in style by embarking on a holiday cruise each year. Whether it's a tropical getaway to the Caribbean or a European river cruise, setting sail together as a family can create unforgettable memories and foster a sense of adventure and togetherness.

Make birthdays extra special by starting the day with a pancake breakfast or by reading a particular book that holds sentimental value to your family. These simple yet meaningful traditions can help your child feel loved and celebrated on their special day.

Escape the hustle and bustle of everyday life with summer trips to natural wonders like Sequoia National Forest or the Grand Canyon. Camping, hiking, and exploring the great outdoors together as a family can create lifelong memories and instill a love of nature in your children.

Expand your horizons with seasonal tours to parts of the United States or abroad. Whether it's a fall foliage tour of New England or a springtime visit to the tulip fields of the Netherlands, these immersive travel experiences can broaden your children's perspectives and create opportunities for cultural exchange and learning.

These are just a few examples of the many ways you can build family traditions that reflect your values, interests, and aspirations. Whether you're embarking on a grand adventure or simply enjoying a quiet evening at home, what matters most is the time spent together and the memories created along the way.

So, embrace the power of traditions in shaping your family's culture and creating lasting bonds that will withstand the test of time. Whether it's an annual holiday cruise, a birthday pancake breakfast, or a summer trip to a national park, these cherished rituals and routines will serve as the foundation for a lifetime of love, connection, and joy.

- ☐ Celebrate the holidays by going on a holiday trip each year.

- ☐ Celebrate birthdays with a pancake breakfast or by reading a particular book.

- ☐ Schedule annual summer trips to national parks.

- ☐ Schedule seasonal tours of different parts of your country or abroad.

- ☐ Read more about creating family traditions: The Book of New Family Traditions: How to Create Great Rituals for Holidays and Every Day and Family Tree Memory Keeper: Your Workbook for Family History, Stories and Genealogy.

CHAPTER 13

TEACHING AND REINFORCING VALUES

Your primary focus should be on teaching your children healthy values, and if your co-parent doesn't hold those values, it's not your responsibility to try to change them or protect them.

This is probably the most important section of this book. These conversations—not lectures—are the cornerstone of raising children who understand and embody healthy values. It's crucial to explicitly teach kids what is acceptable and unacceptable behavior, regardless of whether it paints the toxic person in your life in a bad light. Your primary focus should be on teaching healthy values, and if that person doesn't hold those values, it's not your responsibility to try to change them or protect them.

Here are some important values to establish through conversations with your children:

Safety and Well-being: Teach your children that people should not harm them physically or mentally. Explain that if they ask someone to stop hurting them and that person does not, they should get away from them. Provide examples and ask questions to gauge their understanding. For instance, can someone hit them? Can someone confuse their mind? Can someone tell them that what they saw, heard, or felt didn't happen? How do these things make them feel? Is it okay?

Integrity and Honesty: Instill in your children the importance of having integrity and being true to their word. Discuss when it's acceptable to break a promise, such as in cases of illness or natural disaster.

Consistency and Consideration: Teach your children that words and actions must align, and people should strive to be consistent and considerate of others. Use examples to illustrate the concept, such as cooking meals regularly for a month and then suddenly stopping without explanation.

Respect for Boundaries: Emphasize the importance of respecting boundaries and not trying to manipulate or pressure others into violating their boundaries. Discuss scenarios where someone might try to break their boundaries and how they should respond.

Teaching Conflict Resolution: Teach your children how people deal with conflict and provide them with tools for calming down, such as deep breathing and meditation. Model these techniques yourself and use social-emotional cards to facilitate discussions about healthy ways to handle conflict.

Fostering Self-Awareness and Communication: Use social-emotional cards and emotion identification games to help your children develop self-awareness and effective communication skills. Encourage them to express their feelings openly and teach them how to communicate their needs and boundaries assertively.

Try to find natural moments to insert these values into conversations:

- "People should not harm you physically or mentally."

- "If you ask someone to stop hurting you and they do not, you should get away from them. You do not have to be disrespected by someone who doesn't care about your well-being." Give some examples: "Can someone hit you? Can someone confuse your mind? Can someone tell you that what you saw, heard, or felt didn't happen? How do these things make you feel? Is it ok?"

- "People should have integrity and be true to their word whenever possible. When is it ok to break your word? Only when something makes it impossible for you to uphold your word like an illness or natural disaster."

- "People's words and actions must match. If I say, 'I love you' but I pinch your arm every few minutes, even if you ask me to stop, is that showing love?"

- "People should strive to be consistent. What happens if I cook three meals every day for one month and then, suddenly, I cook nothing at all and say nothing about the change and get angry if you dare to ask me why there's no breakfast before school? Am I being consistent? How would that make you feel? It might make you feel confused."

- "People should be considerate of others. In what ways are you a considerate person?" (Give the child examples of times they have been considerate.)

- "People should be honest. What is honesty? Why is honesty important? Imagine you have a friend who made up stories that never happened and wanted you to believe they were true. Would you believe them the next time they tell you a story? Why not? Would you believe their stories a month from now? A year from now? What would they have to do for you to start believing their stories?"

- "No one should try to break your boundaries. What would happen if you tell me, 'I don't want to give you a hug,' but I start crying or I get angry? Should you feel bad for me and give me a hug even though you don't want to? What I'd be saying is that my feelings matter more than your comfort and your feelings. What if you say 'no' you don't want to give me a hug and I *beg* you to give me a hug and won't take no for an answer? What does that tell you about me? Can I beg you to let me hurt you? Would that be ok? Should you give in?"

By engaging in these conversations and activities, you're not only teaching your children essential life skills but also laying the foundation for healthy relationships and emotional well-being. Remember, these conversations should be ongoing and adapted to suit your children's age and developmental stage. By prioritizing open communication and modeling healthy behaviors yourself, you empower your children to navigate the complexities of life with confidence and resilience.

☐ Consciously teach your children about virtues and values:

o Family Virtues Cards (Virtues Project)

o The Family Virtues Guide: Simple Ways to Bring Out the Best in Our Children and Ourselves

CHAPTER 14
BUILDING SELF-CONFIDENCE AND FEELINGS OF WORTHINESS

Empower your children to advocate for themselves and to feel worthy of good treatment.

Children who are confident and feel worthy of good things are more likely to advocate for themselves, pursue their goals, and navigate challenges with resilience. As parents, we have the power to nurture and strengthen our children's self-esteem through intentional practices and supportive environments.

One way to instill confidence and self-worth in your child is by incorporating affirmations into their daily routine. At the start of each day, take a moment to read an affirmation to your child. Affirmations are positive statements that affirm their strengths, abilities, and worthiness. For example, you might say, "You are capable of achieving anything you set your mind to," or, "You are loved unconditionally just as you are." By starting the day with affirmations, you help your child internalize positive beliefs about themselves and their potential.

In addition to affirmations, visualization exercises can also be powerful tools for building confidence and self-esteem. Each morning or evening, guide your child through a visualization exercise where they imagine themselves succeeding at a specific task or achieving a goal. Encourage them to visualize the details of the experience, including how they feel, what they see, and what they hear. By visualizing success, your child can boost their confidence and develop a positive mindset that empowers them to take on challenges with courage and determination.

Furthermore, the words we speak to our children have a profound impact on their self-image and self-worth. As discussed in an earlier chapter, speaking words of love and encouragement to your child reinforces their sense of worthiness and belonging. By expressing your love and belief in their abilities regularly, you help build a strong foundation of self-esteem that will support them throughout their lives.

By incorporating affirmations, visualization exercises, and words of love into your child's daily routine, you create a nurturing environment where they feel valued, supported, and empowered to advocate for themselves because they feel worthy of good treatment. Remember, building confidence and self-worth is an ongoing process that requires patience, consistency, and unconditional love. As you continue to affirm and support your child, you help them cultivate the inner strength and resilience they need to thrive in an ever-changing world.

Action Items for Your Consideration

☐ At the start of each day, read an affirmation to your child. You can even do so while driving to school.

☐ Do a visualization exercise each morning or at night before bed.

☐ Put affirmation cards in your child's lunchbox each day.

☐ Daily, speak words of love to your child.

☐ Consider adding these affirmation cards and books to your library:

o Daily Positive Affirmation Cards for Kids

o I Believe in Me: A Book of Affirmations

o Imaginations: Fun Relaxation Stories and Meditations for Kids

o Compendium ThoughtFulls for Kids

o Just Because I Am / Solo porque soy yo: A Child's Book of Affirmation

CHAPTER 15

AFFIRMATIONS OF LOVE: NURTURING YOUR CHILD'S HEART AND SOUL

Words have power. Speak only words of love.

As parents, our words hold tremendous power. The things we say to our children shape their self-image, their sense of worth, and their understanding of love and belonging. That's why I make it a point to tell my kids certain things pretty much daily—because these affirmations of love and appreciation are essential for their emotional well-being and development.

Here are some of the things I make sure to tell my kids every day:

"I like you."

"I adore you."

"I love you."

"I not only love you, but I like you."

"I like spending time with you."

"You're a kid, and you're still learning about the world. You're going to make mistakes along the way. It's totally normal for kids to make mistakes or make bad choices until they learn to do better."

"Being with you makes me happy."

"I love snuggling with you."

"Thank you for taking the time to chat with me. I enjoyed our conversation."

"May I have a hug? It's been too long since our last hug."

"You are one of my absolute favorite things in this life."

"You'll never understand how much we love you until you have your own kids, then you'll finally know too."

"You make life beautiful, and I'm glad you exist. The world is better because you're in it."

"My life is better now because you're in it. I'm happier than I ever was before you came along."

These affirmations of love and appreciation are not just words, they're expressions of the deep bond and connection we share with our children. By consistently affirming their worth, their importance in our lives, and our unconditional love for them, we help build a strong foundation of self-esteem and emotional resilience.

We all need to hear these things as children, and truthfully, we all need to hear them as adults too. So, let's not hesitate to shower our children with love, kindness, and affirmations each and every day. After all, there's no limit to the amount of love we can give, and the more we give, the more it grows within us and within our children, enriching our lives and shaping our hearts forever.

CHAPTER 16
CATCH YOUR KIDS DOING THE RIGHT THING

In the hustle and bustle of daily life, it's easy to fall into the habit of correcting our children rather than celebrating their successes. As parents, we often focus on what needs to be fixed, forgetting to acknowledge the countless ways our kids demonstrate kindness, integrity, and resilience throughout their day. However, by actively catching our children doing the right thing, we can shift this narrative and foster a more positive, supportive environment that nurtures their growth.

The Trap of Correction

From the moment they wake up to when they go to bed, children hear a barrage of corrections and criticisms. "Don't forget to brush your teeth!" "Why did you leave your toys out again?" "You shouldn't talk back." While these reminders often come from a place of love and concern, they can unintentionally create a sense of inadequacy. Kids might begin to feel like they are always in trouble or that their worth is tied to their ability to meet adult expectations.

Even the most well-meaning parents can find themselves caught in this cycle. Instead of connecting with their children through praise, they inadvertently reinforce a negative dialogue. This is where the practice of "catching" your kids doing the right thing becomes essential. It helps shift the focus from correction to connection, fostering a healthier and more supportive dynamic.

Celebrating Positive Actions

Imagine the impact of regularly acknowledging the positive behaviors your children display. The more you practice catching them doing the right thing, the easier it becomes to notice and reinforce their good actions.

Here are some examples of what this might look like:

- **Empathy in Action:** "I saw how you comforted your sister when she was upset. You are such an empathetic kid. That was really cool of you!"

- **Integrity Matters:** "Telling the truth is hard, but boy, are you a person of integrity. I appreciate you being honest with me."

- **Self-Control:** "I noticed you took a deep breath to calm yourself instead of hitting or yelling. That took a lot of self-control—more than many adults have. I'm proud of you!"

- **Responsibility Recognized:** "You are so responsible! I appreciate that you followed through on what you said you would do."

- **Persistence Pays Off:** "I see how you kept trying and didn't give up easily, even when you got frustrated. That determination is impressive!"

- **Self-Care:** "Awesome self-care, kiddo! Good for you for taking a break when you felt overwhelmed. That's really smart!"

- **Listening to Their Body:** "I love that you listen to your body and know when you've had enough. That's such an important skill!"

- **Standing Up for Themselves:** "Well done for standing up for yourself today. I'm proud of you!"

Reinforcing Values Through Praise

Each of these statements not only praises your child for their actions but also reinforces the important values you're imparting. By consistently recognizing and validating their positive behaviors, you help them internalize these values, making them a natural part of who they are.

Children are more likely to repeat behaviors that are acknowledged and celebrated. When they see that their kind actions lead to positive reinforcement, they are encouraged to continue those behaviors and, just as importantly, to see those behaviors as normal and natural, and the opposite of those behaviors as anomalous and undesirable. As you work to implement protective factors and establish to your children what healthy behavior is versus unhealthy behavior, normalizing their positive behaviors by catching them doing the right thing is a powerful way to do that.

The Impact on Your Relationship

Beyond cultivating good habits, catching your kids doing the right thing strengthens your relationship with them. When children feel recognized and appreciated, they are more likely to open up and share their thoughts and feelings with you. They sense that you see the best in them, creating a secure emotional bond that encourages trust and communication.

By actively engaging with your children in this positive way, you communicate that you are genuinely interested in their lives and their development. This investment in their well-being goes a long way in helping them feel valued and understood.

Building a New Habit

The practice of catching your kids doing the right thing is not just a one-time effort—it's a habit you should cultivate. The more you actively seek out opportunities to praise your children for their positive behaviors, the more natural it will become. Eventually, you will find that you are consistently highlighting their strengths and good choices, creating a positive atmosphere in your home.

Remember, this is not about ignoring negative behaviors or avoiding necessary corrections. It's about balancing the narrative, ensuring that your children receive equal, if not more, attention for the good they do.

So, take the time to catch your kids doing the right thing. Celebrate their achievements, no matter how small, and reinforce the values you want to instill in them. By focusing on the positive, you will not only help them grow into kind, responsible individuals, but also strengthen your relationship with them. In a world where criticism often overshadows praise, your commitment to recognizing their efforts will make a lasting impact, showing them that they are loved and valued just as they are, and they'll never have a need to seek validation from the wrong people, nor to fill their empty cup from poisonous wells.

Action Items for Your Consideration

☐ Read the book Without Spanking or Spoiling: A Practical Approach to Toddler and Preschool Guidance.

CHAPTER 17

A COMMUNITY OF HEALTH: BUILDING A SUPPORTIVE NETWORK OF ROLE MODELS

These individuals serve as role models, guiding our children by example and reinforcing the lessons we strive to impart at home.

In the journey of raising children, it truly takes a village to instill the values and qualities we hope to see in them. Beyond our immediate family, our children's interactions with a diverse network of individuals can profoundly shape their understanding of healthy relationships, values, and behaviors. These individuals serve as role models, guiding our children by example and reinforcing the lessons we strive to impart at home.

Essentially, this community of intentionally cultivated friends and family should espouse the values discussed in the earlier chapter. They are role models for your kids. Make sure your kids spend time with them regularly. They are helping you to raise your children and showing them how to live a good life.

Here's how you can build a supportive network of role models for your children:

Family and Friends: Encourage regular interactions with family members and close friends who embody the values discussed in the values section of this book. These individuals play a vital role in demonstrating healthy communication, empathy, and respect in relationships.

Mentoring Programs: Look into mentoring programs in your community that pair children with positive adult role models. Mentors can provide guidance, support, and encouragement outside of the family unit, offering unique perspectives and experiences that enrich your child's development.

After-School Programs: Enroll your child in after-school programs that align with their interests and passions. Whether it's art, music, STEM, or sports, these programs provide opportunities for your child to interact with mentors and peers who share similar interests and values.

Extracurricular Clubs: Get involved in clubs such as Scouts, team sports, or other extracurricular activities that promote teamwork, leadership, and personal growth. These clubs offer a supportive community where your child can learn valuable life skills and form meaningful connections with peers and mentors.

Therapists and Counselors: Engage with child therapists or counselors who specialize in developmental and emotional health. These professionals are not only trained to support and guide children through personal challenges but also serve as neutral, compassionate role models. A therapist can provide a safe space for your child to explore their feelings, develop coping strategies, and reinforce the values of self-awareness and emotional resilience. Regular sessions can help your child understand and manage their emotions effectively, fostering a deeper sense of self-understanding and confidence.

Incorporating this into the broader context of building a support network emphasizes the importance of professional guidance alongside community and familial support, rounding out the diverse range of influences that contribute to your child's development.

By actively seeking out opportunities for your child to engage with positive role models in various settings, you provide them with a rich and diverse support system that complements the values and principles you instill at home. These role models not only reinforce the lessons you teach but also offer unique perspectives and experiences that contribute to your child's growth and development.

Remember, raising children is a collaborative effort, and by nurturing a network of supportive role models, you empower your child to navigate the complexities of life with confidence, resilience, and integrity. So, invest in these relationships, cultivate connections, and celebrate the village of individuals who contribute to your child's journey towards becoming their best selves.

☐ Look into mentoring programs such as Big Brothers Big Sisters.

☐ Look into afterschool programs such as the Boys & Girls Clubs of America.

☐ Look into family activity programs such as Jack and Jill of America.

☐ Work with your insurance or employee assistance program to secure a therapist for your child.

☐ Work with your child's school counselor to schedule regular sessions with your child.

☐ Get your child involved in clubs such as Boy Scouts of America, Girl Scouts of America, The Baden-Powell Scouts' Association, team sports, individual sports such as martial arts, band, or other extracurriculars.

CHAPTER 18

ENSURING COMMUNICATION AND SAFETY AT THE CO-PARENT'S HOUSE

Empower your children with the means to communicate with you to advocate for their safety.

When your children spend time at their co-parent's house, ensuring their safety and well-being remains a top priority. To facilitate open communication and provide them with the support they need, it's essential to equip them with the tools and resources necessary to reach out to you in case of trouble or confusion. Here are the essentials you should consider for your children when they go to their co-parent's house:

1. **Cell Phone or Video Call Ability:** Ensure that your children have access to a cell phone or the ability to contact you via FaceTime or other video call platforms. This allows them to reach out to you quickly and easily, regardless of their location or circumstances.

2. **Establish Nightly Check-Ins:** Consider asking your children to call you nightly or vice versa. This regular check-in provides an opportunity for them to share any concerns or updates about their day, reinforcing the importance of communication and connection.

3. **Emergency Contacts:** Review and update the list of emergency contacts with your children before they go to their co-parent's house. Make sure they know who to contact in case of an emergency and how to get help if needed. Refer to the Community of Health section for guidance on compiling a comprehensive list of emergency contacts.

4. **Encourage Open Communication:** Encourage your children to call, text, or FaceTime you any time they feel confused or need help while at their co-parent's house. Assure them that you are always available to listen, mediate, and advocate for them on the spot. Remind them that it's okay to reach out for help and that you are proud of their bravery and confidence in doing so.

Bravery and Confidence: Acknowledge that reaching out for help may require bravery and confidence, but reassure your children that they are up to the task. Remind them of their strength and resilience, and emphasize that you believe in their ability to navigate challenging situations.

Validating Your Child's Reality: Recognize that you may not be able to change your co-parent's perspective, but you can validate your child's reality and experiences. By listening to their concerns and offering support, you help them feel heard, understood, and supported.

By empowering your children with the means to communicate with you and advocating for their safety and well-being, you demonstrate your unwavering commitment to their happiness and security. By fostering open communication and providing a supportive network, you create a safe and nurturing environment for your children to thrive, even in the face of challenging circumstances. Remember, you are their advocate and ally, and your dedication to their welfare is unwavering.

☐ Consider giving your child an age-appropriate phone, such as a Gabb phone, so that they can contact you when with their other parent.

CHAPTER 19
GETTING READY FOR THE NEXT VISIT

Prepare your child for what they might encounter during their upcoming visit.

As the time approaches for your child's next visit with their other parent, consider the disagreements and tensions that may have surfaced between you and your co-parent since the last visit. Perhaps they've asked for additional visitation days or requested a change in the schedule that you had to decline. Maybe they've been resistant to an extracurricular activity you want your child to participate in or have refused to allow your child to attend therapy. Whatever the issues may be, it's critical to prepare your child for what they might encounter during their upcoming visit.

Anticipating Challenges

Your child may encounter subtle pressure or suggestions from their other parent regarding any contentious matters between you and your co-parent. The other parent might attempt to put your child in the middle of your conflict, so it's important to address this possibility proactively and equip your child with the tools they need to handle such conversations.

One way to do this is by having a brief, mature discussion with your child about the topics they might hear about from their co-parent during their visit. You can explain that their other parent may want to discuss specific issues, such as visitation schedules or extracurricular activities, but emphasize that these conversations are best handled between the adults. Let your child know that it is not their responsibility to mediate or carry messages between you and their other parent.

Empowering Your Child with Words

To empower your child, provide them with specific phrases they can use to set boundaries. Encourage them to say things like, "I don't want to talk about this. Please talk to my dad about that," or, "That's a conversation best had with my mom," or, "I don't want to be in the middle of this, so please talk to my dad about that." They might also feel comfortable using their own wording, so encourage them to rephrase your suggestions. Role-playing scenarios where you bring up a topic and your child responds using the phrases you've suggested can make this feel more natural for them.

This practice not only builds their confidence but also reinforces the idea that they have the right to assert their boundaries. It teaches them that they can navigate conversations with their other parent without feeling overwhelmed or responsible for the dynamics between you two.

Providing On-the-Spot Support

In the event that your child finds themselves in a situation where their other parent disregards their boundaries and insists on discussing inappropriate topics or making them the go-between, reassure them that they can reach out to you or other adults in your trusted support network for immediate backing. Encouraging your child to call you or a trusted adult if they feel uncomfortable or pressured reminds them that they have someone to turn to in times of distress and that it's important to protect their emotional well-being.

Striking a Delicate Balance

Finding the balance between preparing your child for the potential challenges they might face and avoiding triangulation is delicate but essential. The goal is not to instill fear or anxiety about their visit but to equip them with tools and strategies to handle whatever comes their way. With the right preparation, your child can approach their next visit with confidence, ready to engage in healthy boundaries while enjoying the positive aspects of their time with their other parent.

CHAPTER 20

GOING-AWAY RITUALS: TRANSITIONING TO THE OTHER PARENT'S HOUSE

These rituals not only help ease the transition between households but also reinforce your bond with your children.

As a co-parent, one of the most challenging aspects of sharing custody is helping your children navigate the transition between households. Going-away rituals provide a comforting and reassuring way to help ease this transition and reinforce your connection with your children. Here are some rituals to consider implementing when your children are preparing to go to the other parent's house:

1. **Snuggle Time:** Spend some quiet, quality time together snuggling on the couch or in bed. Use this time to bond, share affection, and create a sense of closeness before parting ways.

2. **Sing or Listen to a Song:** Choose a special song, such as "Until I See You Again," to listen to or sing together. Music has a powerful way of evoking emotions and can serve as a comforting reminder of your love and connection.

3. **Read Books Together:** Curl up with your children and read their favorite books together. Reading together not only promotes literacy but also provides an opportunity for bonding and relaxation.

4. **Meditate Together:** Practice a short meditation or mindfulness exercise together to help calm any anxieties or worries about the transition. Encourage your children to focus on their breath and cultivate a sense of inner peace and tranquility.

5. **Remind Them to Call:** Reinforce the importance of communication by reminding your children that they can and should call you if they need you while they're away. Assure them that you'll always be there to listen, support, and help them navigate any challenges.

6. **Goodnight Calls:** Arrange for nightly calls to say goodnight or encourage your children to call you before bedtime. This ritual provides a sense of continuity and connection, even when you're apart.

7. **Believe Their Own Mind:** Remind your children to trust their instincts and believe in their own perceptions and experiences. Encourage them to speak up if something doesn't feel right and assure them that their feelings are valid and important.

8. **Express Love and Excitement:** Before they leave, remind your children that you had a wonderful time with them while they were with you and express your excitement for their return. Reassure them of your love and anticipation for their homecoming.

9. **Encourage Enjoyment:** Remind your children to enjoy themselves with the other parent and make the most of their time together. Emphasize the importance of cherishing happy moments and creating positive memories.

10. **Take the Good, Leave the Bad:** Encourage your children to focus on the positive aspects of their time with the other parent and to not incorporate into their identity any of the bad behaviors they may witness or be victim to. Remind them that they have the power to choose how they respond to their circumstances. This isn't meant to suggest they should intentionally forget the bad things that happen to them. It is to encourage them to see the bad behaviors as examples of things they should not aspire to, while encouraging them to enjoy the good aspects of their other parent.

11. **Greatest Ally Reminder:** Lastly, remind your children that you are their greatest ally and advocate. Assure them that you will always be there to support and protect them, no matter where they are or what challenges they face.

By incorporating these going-away rituals into your co-parenting routine, you provide your children with a sense of stability, love, and connection during times of transition. These rituals not only help ease the transition between households but also reinforce your bond with your children and strengthen their sense of security and well-being. Remember, consistency and reassurance are key, and by prioritizing your children's emotional needs, you create a foundation for healthy co-parenting and positive relationships for years to come.

CHAPTER 21

RITUALS FOR RETURNING HOME: CREATING WARMTH AND COMFORT

*Embrace return-home rituals as opportunities
to strengthen your family bond.*

Returning home after time spent away can be a mixed experience for children. While they may be excited to reunite with familiar surroundings and loved ones, they may also feel a sense of apprehension or uncertainty about reentering the routines of daily life. As a parent, establishing return-home rituals can help ease this transition and create a sense of warmth, comfort, and security for your children.

Return-home rituals are an essential part of your family culture, providing a familiar and comforting routine that helps your children feel settled back into the fold of health. These rituals don't need to involve extravagant gestures or material rewards; instead, they focus on simple yet meaningful ways to welcome your children back into the home environment.

Here are some suggestions for return-home rituals:

1. **Welcome with a Smile and a Hug:** Greet your children with open arms and a warm smile as soon as they walk through the door. There's nothing quite like the comfort of a loving embrace to make your children feel valued and cherished.

2. **Express How You Missed Them:** Tell your children, "I'm so glad you're home. I missed you." Hearing these words reassures your children that they were missed and that their presence is appreciated and valued.

3. **Read a Book Together:** Settle in for some cozy family time by reading a book together. Choose a favorite story or let your children pick one that they've been eager to read. Snuggle up together and lose yourselves in the pages of a good book.

4. **Snuggle Time:** Take a moment to snuggle up with your children and enjoy some quiet time together. Use this time to reconnect, share stories about your day, and reaffirm your bond with one another.

These return-home rituals provide your children with a sense of comfort, stability, and belonging as they transition back into the familiar rhythms of home life. By prioritizing connection and emotional well-being over material rewards, you reinforce the importance of relationships and shared experiences in your family culture.

Remember, it's the simple gestures of love and affection that leave a lasting impression on your children's hearts. By welcoming them home with open arms, kind words, and meaningful rituals, you create a nurturing and supportive environment where they feel valued, loved, and secure. So, embrace these return-home rituals as opportunities to strengthen your family bond and create lasting memories together.

- ☐ Welcome your kids with a smile and a hug—who doesn't like to receive a smile upon sight?

- ☐ Tell your kids, "I'm so glad you're home. I missed you," as soon as they arrive home.

- ☐ Read a book together.

- ☐ Snuggle up and have a moment of calm together.

CHAPTER 22
POST-VISIT DEBRIEF

Navigating co-parenting with a toxic ex-partner can be emotionally challenging, especially when it comes to debriefing with your children after visits. It's essential to approach these conversations with care and sensitivity, prioritizing your children's emotional well-being while also holding space for their reality.

We are not trying to villainize the other parent. We simply want to hold the space of reality for our children. We do not want them to get sucked into the vortex of confusion and identity loss that being around a toxic person can cause. We remind our children that we see them, we validate their experience, and we hold the space of reality with and for them. We help them feel like some things are just and other things are unjust.

The aim of debrief sessions is to help your children process their experiences in a healthy and constructive manner. By acknowledging and validating their feelings, you create a safe space for them to express themselves openly and honestly.

Here are some key principles to keep in mind during post-visit debriefs with the toxic co-parent:

1. **Validate Their Experience:** Start by acknowledging your children's feelings and experiences without judgment or criticism. Let them know that it's okay to feel whatever they're feeling and that you're here to listen and support them.

2. **Hold the Space of Reality:** Remind your children that you see them and validate their reality. Help them distinguish between what is just and unjust, acknowledging the challenges they may face when interacting with the toxic co-parent.

3. **Avoid Villainizing the Other Parent:** While it's essential to address any concerning behaviors or dynamics, refrain from demonizing the other parent in front of your children. Instead, focus on helping them understand and process their experiences in a healthy and constructive manner.

4. **Remind Them to Take the Good and Leave the Bad:** Encourage your child to take the good and leave the bad when it comes to their other parent. Help them acknowledge the negative patterns, habits, and choices that may exist, reinforcing the importance of recognizing these behaviors to protect themselves from harm. However, remind them that few people are entirely bad—there may be moments or qualities worth appreciating.

5. **Provide Reassurance and Support:** Offer reassurance and support to your children, emphasizing that they are not alone in navigating these challenging situations. Remind them that you are here for them, and that together, you will find ways to cope and move forward.

6. **Encourage Open Communication:** Foster open communication with your children, encouraging them to express their thoughts, feelings, and concerns freely. Listen attentively to what they have to say, and validate their experiences with empathy and understanding.

7. **Focus on Building Resilience:** Use these debriefs as an opportunity to teach your children coping skills and resilience-building strategies. Help them develop healthy boundaries, assertiveness, and self-care practices to navigate interactions with the toxic co-parent more effectively.

Ultimately, post-visit debriefs with the toxic co-parent serve as a vital opportunity to support your children's emotional well-being and help them navigate the complexities of co-parenting with a challenging ex-partner. By approaching these conversations with empathy, understanding, and a focus on validation and support, you create a safe and nurturing environment where your children feel seen, heard, and valued. Remember, your role as a parent is to guide and support your children through life's challenges and post-visit debriefs are just one way to fulfill that essential responsibility with love and compassion.

CHAPTER 23

TELL THE TRUTH WITHOUT BAD-MOUTHING

It's crucial to foster healthy boundaries regarding discussions about the other parent.

One of the most delicate balances to strike in co-parenting with a toxic ex-partner is telling the truth to your children about the dynamics of the relationship without resorting to bad-mouthing or demonizing the other parent. It's essential to maintain integrity and honesty while also protecting your children from unnecessary emotional harm.

Fostering Healthy Boundaries

As a parent, it's crucial to foster healthy boundaries regarding discussions about the other parent. Let your children know that while they can and should talk to you about their feelings, it's important not to demonize their other parent and that parents can and do make mistakes. This is a difficult balance to strike because, while we don't want to absolve the other parent of their legitimate wrongdoings, we also don't want to encourage your child to make the other parent a punching bag. You might explain, "It's okay to talk about how you feel, but we should also remember that your other parent often tries to do their best," or, "Your other parent may not be good at communicating without yelling, but it seems like they are trying to yell less often lately."

This approach reinforces the idea that it's acceptable to have feelings but also highlights the importance of maintaining a balanced perspective for both parents rather than seeing one parent as "the bad guy." It also teaches children that they can navigate complex emotions without resorting to a habit of perpetual negative talk about either parent.

Modeling Healthy Communication

You set the tone for how your children communicate about their other parent. If your child brings up an issue related to their other parent, approach it with empathy and understanding. Avoid making negative comments about the other parent, even if you feel justified. Instead, focus on providing guidance and support.

For instance, if your child says something negative about their other parent, you might respond, "I understand you're upset. Let's figure out how we can make things better. What would help you feel more comfortable? How can I support you?" This allows your child to express their feelings while steering the conversation toward constructive solutions.

Teaching Emotional Intelligence

One of the best ways to handle your child's feelings about their other parent is to encourage emotional intelligence. Help your child understand that it's natural to feel a range of emotions about both parents, including love, frustration, and confusion. Instead of framing their feelings as a conflict between two sides, teach them that it's possible to love both parents while also feeling hurt or upset by certain behaviors.

Encourage them to express their feelings openly and help them articulate what they are experiencing. You can ask open-ended questions like, "What made you feel that way?" or, "How do you think we can solve this together?" This not only validates their feelings but also teaches them healthy communication skills.

Here are some strategies for telling the truth without bad-mouthing:

1. **Focus on Values and Boundaries:** When discussing the reasons for the separation or the challenges in the relationship with your ex, focus on values and boundaries. You can explain to your children that you and your ex had different values or that certain boundaries were not respected. Emphasize the importance of mutual respect and healthy communication in any relationship.

2. **Avoid Specific Details:** Refrain from delving into specific details or incidents from the past relationship that may be hurtful or inappropriate for your children to hear. Instead, keep the conversation general and focus on broader concepts such as respect, honesty, and integrity.

3. **Use Age-Appropriate Language:** Tailor your explanations to the age and maturity level of your children. Use language that they can understand and process, avoiding complex or adult concepts that may be confusing or distressing for them.

4. **Empower Your Children:** When your children come to you with complaints about their other parent and it is an issue that is clearly one of toxicity but doesn't rise to the level of requiring police intervention (like the child has experienced gaslighting, name-calling, etc.), ask them questions like: "Based on our values, is that an appropriate way to behave?" "How might you have handled that situation if you were the adult?" "What would you like me to do? How can I support you?"

5. **Provide Support and Validation:** Offer your children support and validation for their feelings and experiences. Let them know that it's okay to feel upset or confused and that you are here to listen and support them unconditionally.

6. **Seek Their Input:** Involve your children in decision-making processes and ask for their input on how to handle certain situations. Empower them to express their needs and preferences, and work together to find solutions that are in their best interests.

By approaching conversations about the other parent with honesty, integrity, and sensitivity, you can help your children navigate the complexities of co-parenting with a toxic ex-partner while also preserving their emotional well-being. Remember, your role as a parent is to guide and support your children with love and compassion, even in the face of challenging circumstances. By prioritizing their needs and feelings, you create a safe and nurturing environment where they can thrive and grow emotionally.

CHAPTER 24

BEING YOUR CHILD'S ALLY IN CO-PARENTING

Your child will feel loved and protected knowing that they have someone who is truly in their corner.

The most crucial role you can assume is that of your child's ally. Your child should know, without a doubt, that they have someone in their corner, someone who is unwaveringly supportive and protective of their well-being. However, to be an effective ally, you must navigate the delicate waters of communication with your co-parent carefully.

Keep Complaints Private

First and foremost, it's essential to avoid complaining about your child to your co-parent. Sharing your frustrations can seem tempting, especially when tensions are running high between you and your child, but it's a practice that can backfire significantly. Your co-parent is not your friend, and any grievances you share can be weaponized against you or, worse, against your child.

Imagine a scenario where you express frustration about your child's behavior—perhaps they're having difficulty with their schoolwork, or you feel annoyed by how much your child whined and complained on a recent vacation. Your co-parent might take that complaint and turn it into a punitive measure, saying something like, "Your mom also thinks you're ungrateful!" Such statements can damage your child's trust and belief in you as their ally, making them feel unsupported.

Focus on Solutions

Instead of participating in a venting session about your child with your co-parent, aim to reframe the conversation. If your co-parent begins to whine or complain about your child, guide the dialogue toward solutions. Help them understand what is developmentally appropriate for your child's age and behavior.

For example, if your child is acting out because they're tired, gently remind your co-parent that children often struggle with their emotions when they haven't had enough rest. You might say, "I've noticed that when they don't nap, they tend to get cranky. Maybe we could both work on ensuring they have some downtime."

By steering the conversation toward understanding and solutions, you are reinforcing the idea that your child is not a problem to be fixed but a developing individual whose actions can be explained and supported.

Educate About Developmental Stages

It's also important to respond to complaints by educating your co-parent about developmental stages and the reasons behind your child's actions. Many behaviors that may seem frustrating are entirely normal for children at different ages. For instance, toddlers are known for their tantrums, and preschoolers are often learning to navigate social interactions. Remind your co-parent that some behaviors are part of growing up, not indications of poor parenting or ungratefulness.

If your co-parent expresses concerns about your child's behavior, you could respond with, "That's a normal phase for their age. Kids often test boundaries as they learn what's acceptable." This approach fosters a dialogue that is more supportive of your child.

Protect Your Child's Emotional Safety

Your child needs to feel secure in the knowledge that you are there to protect and advocate for them. Remind them that they can come to you with anything they are feeling and reassure them that they are loved unconditionally.

It's vital to create an environment where your child feels comfortable expressing their feelings about *both* parents—this includes being open to hearing your child's criticisms of you. If they feel safe sharing all of their thoughts, they are less likely to internalize any negative comments or feelings that might arise from interactions with the other parent. Validate their feelings by saying things like, "It's okay to feel frustrated sometimes. I understand and have felt that way before. It makes sense that you'd feel frustrated by what you experienced."

Maintaining a Protective Stance

Ultimately, your role is to create a protective factor for your child, shielding them from the negative influences of a toxic co-parent. This means reinforcing that they have an advocate in you. Make it clear that your child can always rely on you for support, even when things get tough.

By prioritizing your child's emotional safety, focusing on solutions rather than grievances, and educating your co-parent about appropriate developmental behaviors, you are solidifying your position as your child's ally.

In co-parenting, it's easy to fall into a cycle of negativity and blame, but by staying focused on being a supportive force in your child's life, you create an environment where they can thrive. They will feel loved and protected, knowing that they have someone who is truly in their corner, no matter what challenges arise.

CHAPTER 25
KEEPING YOUR CHILDREN'S TRUST

Maintaining the confidentiality of your child's feelings and avoiding triangulation builds a strong foundation of trust.

In the delicate landscape of co-parenting, one of the most significant responsibilities you hold as a parent is to be a trustworthy confidant for your children. They may share their feelings, concerns, or experiences about their other parent with you, and it's crucial to handle this information with care. Maintaining this trust not only reinforces your bond with your child but also helps protect them from the emotional turmoil that can arise from triangulation.

The Importance of Confidentiality

When your children confide in you about their experiences with their co-parent, they are expressing vulnerability. This trust is a gift; it means they feel safe with you and believe that you will listen without judgment. It is vital to honor this confidentiality. Avoid sharing these sensitive conversations with the other parent as doing so can betray your child's trust and lead to feelings of insecurity and confusion.

For example, if your child expresses frustration about a situation with their other parent, resist the urge to relay this information back to your co-parent. Sharing this can inadvertently turn your child into a pawn in the ongoing conflict, causing them to feel caught in the middle. Instead, reassure your child that their feelings are valid and that they can speak freely without fear of repercussions.

Avoiding Triangulation

Triangulation occurs when one parent uses their child to relay messages or express grievances about the other parent. This can create an unhealthy dynamic, making your child feel responsible for adult conflicts. It's essential to avoid putting your child in this position.

When your co-parent expresses frustration or engages in negative talk about you, it can be tempting to share your side of the story with your child. However, this can create confusion and guilt for your child, making them feel like they must choose sides. Instead, focus on remaining neutral and supportive. You might say something like, "I understand you're feeling confused and upset. It makes complete sense to feel that way and I understand. Let's talk about how we can help you feel better about the situation."

Building Trust for the Future

Ultimately, maintaining the confidentiality of your child's feelings and avoiding triangulation builds a strong foundation of trust. When your child knows they can share their thoughts and emotions without fear of repercussion or judgment, they are more likely to come to you with their feelings in the future. This trust is vital in helping them navigate the complexities of their relationships and emotions.

By being a reliable ally and confidant, you are not only supporting your child but also modeling healthy behavior that they can carry into their adult relationships. They will learn the value of trust, empathy, and open communication—skills that will serve them well throughout their lives.

CHAPTER 26

NAVIGATING A CHILD'S CONFLICTING EMOTIONS ABOUT THEIR OTHER PARENT

Just because their other parent has exhibited negative or harmful behaviors doesn't mean your child will stop loving them.

One of the most challenging aspects of co-parenting, especially with a toxic or narcissistic ex, is managing your child's conflicting emotions about their other parent. It can be confusing and difficult for a child to process, and it can be equally challenging for you to support them through these emotions. Your child may vacillate between anger at their other parent, refusing to see them, and moments of longing, missing them deeply and wanting to spend time with them. This emotional push and pull is normal, even when the other parent has exhibited abusive behavior or substance abuse issues. Children naturally want to love both parents, even if one of them has caused harm.

Conflicting Feelings Are Normal

It's important to first understand that your child's conflicting feelings are entirely normal. Just because their other parent has exhibited negative or harmful behaviors doesn't mean your child will stop loving them. Even in cases of abuse or substance addiction, children can still pine for the connection they feel with that parent. They may feel anger, hurt, or confusion, but they also have a deep desire to maintain that bond. This is a natural and normal part of the human experience.

This can be incredibly confusing for your child. They may feel that it's wrong to love someone who has caused them or you pain, or they might feel guilty for their anger. As a parent, your role is to validate both emotions. Let your child know that it's okay to feel both love and anger at the same time. Those two feelings can exist side by side, and it doesn't mean that their love is wrong or that their anger is unjustified.

You might say something like, "It's okay to feel upset with your other parent, and it's also okay to miss them. Both of those feelings are completely normal." By normalizing these conflicting emotions, you're giving your child the space to process their feelings without guilt or confusion.

It's Okay Not to Dwell on the Bad Behavior

While it's important for your child to express their feelings about the other parent, it's also important to help them avoid dwelling on every negative experience. Constantly revisiting the hurtful actions of the other parent can keep them stuck in a cycle of anger or resentment. Encourage your child to acknowledge their experiences without allowing those experiences to dominate their thoughts.

That doesn't mean brushing the bad behavior under the rug or pretending it didn't happen. Instead, it means encouraging your child to cast those negative experiences aside with a tether to them. They shouldn't feel pressured to carry the burden of constantly reliving their pain, but they also shouldn't completely forget the lessons those experiences have taught them.

You might tell your child, "We don't have to keep thinking about everything that went wrong, but it's okay to hold onto what we've learned from it." This gives them permission to move forward without erasing the past.

Noticing Patterns of Behavior for Safety

While it's important not to dwell on every negative experience, it's equally important to help your child notice patterns of behavior. These patterns are key to keeping themselves emotionally and physically safe. By recognizing how the other parent's behavior affects them, they can learn to anticipate and navigate difficult situations without being blindsided.

For example, if the other parent has a pattern of making promises and then not following through, your child can begin to recognize that pattern without holding onto constant disappointment. They might still miss their other parent, but they'll learn to take promises with caution rather than setting themselves up for emotional hurt every time.

Encourage your child to notice these patterns gently. You could say, "It's important to remember how things usually go with your other parent, not because we want to be upset, but so we can protect ourselves from being hurt again."

By noticing these patterns, your child will develop a stronger sense of emotional resilience. They won't feel like they're falling into the same trap over and over again, and they'll learn to approach their relationship with the other parent with more awareness and self-protection.

Finding Balance in Love and Boundaries

Ultimately, your goal as a parent is to help your child find balance. It's okay for them to love their other parent, and it's okay for them to be angry. They should also feel safe in setting boundaries that protect their emotional well-being. The conflicting emotions they feel are a natural part of navigating a difficult family dynamic, and your role is to guide them through those emotions without making them feel guilty or confused.

By helping your child understand that it's normal to feel both love and anger, encouraging them not to dwell on the past, and teaching them to notice patterns of behavior, you're giving them the tools they need to manage their relationship with their other parent in a healthy way. It's not an easy path, but with your support, they'll learn to navigate these challenges with strength and awareness, keeping themselves safe emotionally while allowing room for love and connection where appropriate.

CHAPTER 27

REMINDING YOUR CHILD OF THEIR JOB DESCRIPTION

Reinforce to your child that children are worthy of care and safety and that their well-being should always come first.

As a parent navigating the complexities of co-parenting, one of the most challenging emotions to address is your child's fear of getting their other parent in trouble. Children often feel torn between their love for both parents and the instinct to protect the adult who has let them down. It's crucial to help them understand that while love for a parent is natural, their responsibility lies not in shielding adults from the consequences of their actions, but in prioritizing their own well-being.

Understanding Consequences

The first step in addressing this concern is to teach your children about consequences. Explain to them that every action has repercussions—both good and bad. When adults, including their other parent, engage in behavior that causes harm or distress, it's essential to recognize that those actions are unacceptable. Remind them that it's not their job to protect an adult from the consequences of their wrongdoing. It's the responsibility of both parents to ensure their children feel safe and cared for.

You might say something like, "It's important to understand that if someone is hurting you or making you feel unsafe, you have the right to speak up. It's not your job to protect adults who are not doing their part to keep you safe." This message reinforces the idea that children are worthy of care and safety and that their well-being should always come first.

Absolve Them of Adult Responsibilities

Next, it's crucial to absolve your children of the responsibility of taking care of an adult's feelings or safety. Being a child means having the freedom to enjoy life, explore, and feel secure in their environment. Their job is to be a kid—playing, learning, and growing—while your role is to handle the difficult work of ensuring their safety and well-being.

You can reinforce this idea by saying, "You don't have to worry about making your other parent feel better or keeping them safe. That's my job as your parent. Your job is to enjoy being a kid and know that I will always do my best to protect you." This assurance helps alleviate their fears and allows them to focus on being children, free from the weight of adult concerns.

Prioritizing Their Well-Being

It's essential to make it clear that if someone is failing in their role as a parent—especially in ways that cause your child harm—such behavior cannot be tolerated. You're teaching them to recognize when actions are inappropriate or hurtful and emphasize that it's perfectly acceptable to voice their feelings about those situations. Reiterate that their feelings matter, and they should feel empowered to express discomfort or fear without guilt.

Additionally, reassure your child that you are committed to addressing any issues that arise with the co-parent. Emphasize that you will do your best to communicate and resolve problems without involving them or putting them in the middle. You might say, "If there's something that needs to be addressed with your other parent, I will handle it. You don't have to worry about what happens or feel responsible for keeping anyone safe. Your feelings are important to me, and I will take care of this like a responsible parent should."

Creating a Safe Space

Ultimately, your goal is to create a safe space where your children feel valued, heard, and protected. Reassure them that your primary responsibility is to look out for their well-being and that they can trust you to handle difficult situations. Remind them that they are worthy of love and care, and your commitment to them is unwavering.

By instilling these values, you help your children develop a healthy understanding of boundaries, responsibilities, and the importance of self-care. They will learn that while love for both parents is natural, it should never come at the expense of their safety or emotional well-being. This foundation will empower them to build strong relationships and navigate life's challenges with resilience and confidence.

CHAPTER 28

THE DEFAULT IS NO

Allowing your co-parent more access to your child sends a powerful message to your child: their other parent's unacceptable behaviors are actually acceptable.

It's not uncommon for children to crave additional time with the harmful parent, often due to love bombing or manipulative tactics that distort their perception of reality. In these moments, it's vital to remember that your default response should generally be "no," unless there are compelling reasons to say otherwise—like your own illness that renders you unable to care for your children, or a business trip that cannot be cancelled.

Allowing your co-parent more access to your child can open the door to further manipulation, confusion, and emotional harm. Every extra hour your child spends with a problematic co-parent is another opportunity for that parent to use their manipulation tools. And giving your co-parent more time with your child sends a powerful message to your child: that their other parent's unacceptable behaviors are actually acceptable, undermining the protective factors you have worked hard to establish.

We must earnestly recognize that not all co-parenting arrangements are beneficial for children. Despite the family court's emphasis on the importance of both parents being equally involved, many adults reflect on their upbringing with regret, wishing they had received guidance and support in navigating a harmful relationship with a mentally unstable parent. It's widely accepted that childhood personalities are largely formed by about age seven, heavily influenced by their environment and the role models around them. This makes it all the more important to cultivate an atmosphere that aligns with your family's mission, vision, and values—one that prioritizes emotional health and stability.

Whether it's that your other parent has asked for more time with your child, or your child wants more time with their other parent, it's an opportunity to gently educate your child about the dynamics at play. You can acknowledge their feelings while also reinforcing the importance of boundaries and healthy relationships. For instance, you might say, "I understand you want to spend more time with your mom, but it's important for us to follow the parenting plan she and I agreed upon."

The Risks of Precedent

Be mindful that in some jurisdictions, if one parent consistently allows more time with the other, it could set a precedent that the courts might recognize. This can lead to the other parent successfully requesting increased custody or parenting time based on the established pattern of access. Therefore, be careful about any additional time granted outside the boundaries of your custody agreement.

Your approach to parenting time should be calculated and deliberate. Communicate clearly with your child about why you're declining their request. You might explain, "Your dad and I agreed to our parenting plan, and it's important that we follow it." This reinforces the idea that both parents are bound by legal agreements, and it helps your child understand that boundaries exist for their protection.

Building a Healthy Foundation

By holding firm on the default "no" for extra time with a harmful parent, you create a safer environment for your child to grow up in, and doing so helps them learn that love and connection can coexist with boundaries.

CHAPTER 29
PRACTICE TIME: RUNNING SCENARIOS

Practice makes perfect, they say, and this rings true even in the realm of advocating for oneself, especially in the context of co-parenting with a toxic individual. By engaging in scenario practice sessions with your children, you not only empower them to stand up for themselves but also provide yourself with valuable opportunities to respond calmly and effectively to their needs.

The following scenario practice suggestions are not just for your children, they are also for you to get used to hearing your children advocate for themselves and give you an opportunity to practice responding calmly rather than seeing it as "back talk." This teaches your children that they have the right to stand up for themselves when they are wronged.

It's important for you to explain to your child that you are giving them examples and practicing so that they can learn how to respond. You can even make this fun by making the scenarios outlandish by using fantasy elements. For example, "Imagine I'm a troll but I try to make you believe I'm a princess and I get angry with you because you keep pointing out that I'm a troll," or anything else you think might tickle your child's fancy.

Here are some scenario practice suggestions to consider:

1. **"No, Thank You":** Role-play situations where your child asserts their boundaries by saying, "No, thank you," when they feel uncomfortable or violated. For example, if you tickle your child without consent, and they say, "No, thank you," acknowledge their boundary and respect their decision. You can even respond, "Ok. I'll stop because it's your body." By responding positively, you teach your child how a healthy person should respond to their boundaries.

2. **"Please Stop":** Practice scenarios where your child communicates discomfort or displeasure, and you respond calmly and respectfully. Encourage them to assert themselves by saying, "Please stop," and model appropriate ways to handle their request without escalating the situation. For instance, you tell your child you don't like something they've done and you start to get worked up and angry as you talk with them. In response, your child says, "Please stop." You take a deep breath and reply that you're going to take a break and return to the conversation when you're calmer. You can even thank them for saying that they were feeling uncomfortable with the conversation. In this way, you build your child's self-advocacy muscle.

3. **Begging, Badgering, Boundary-Breaking:** Explore scenarios in which your child has said, "Not right now," to you when you've asked for a hug. You then start begging them by saying, "Pleeeease, just one quick hug?", emotionally manipulating them by looking sad and pouting, pretending to cry and crying on command to manipulate them into giving you a hug, berating them to shame them into giving you a hug, giving them the silent

treatment to manipulate them into giving you a hug, or storming off angrily to manipulate them into giving you a hug. Encourage your child to be firm about their boundaries as you run through each scenario. Because your tantrum has nothing to do with them.

4. **Trusting Their Reality:** Practice scenarios where your child asserts their perception of reality, even when challenged by others. For instance, practice a scenario in which your child sees a plane fly by but you tell them, no that wasn't a plane, that was a bird. Although sometimes we can get things wrong and our mind can occasionally play tricks on us, if your child is confident about their reality, encourage your child to say, "I'm confident that I saw what I saw," and, "Let's talk about something else." Remind them to believe their own mind. Remind them that you are their greatest ally and advocate.

By engaging in scenario practice sessions with your children, you empower them to assert their boundaries, advocate for themselves, and trust their own perceptions. These sessions also provide you with valuable opportunities to model healthy communication and conflict resolution skills, ultimately fostering a supportive and empowering environment for your children to thrive. Remember, practice may not make perfect, but it certainly makes progress, and every step forward counts.

CHAPTER 30
REINFORCING AND PRACTICING

Consistency is key when it comes to reinforcing and practicing healthy behaviors and boundaries with your children. While scenario practice sessions at home provide valuable opportunities for learning and growth, it's essential to continue reinforcing these lessons in real-life situations.

Here are some strategies for reinforcing and practicing healthy behaviors with your children:

1. **Scenario Practice Continues:** Keep the momentum going by incorporating scenario practice into your daily routines. Whether you're at home, in the car, or out and about, seize opportunities to engage in role-play discussions with your children. Use real-life situations as teaching moments to reinforce the importance of setting boundaries and advocating for oneself.

2. **Discussing Bad Behavior:** When you witness inappropriate or unhealthy behavior in public, use it as an opportunity to engage in meaningful discussions with your children. Prompt them to reflect on what they observed and discuss why certain behaviors are not

acceptable. Encourage open dialogue and critical thinking as you explore these topics together.

3. **Consistent Communication:** Maintain open lines of communication with your children about their experiences and challenges. Encourage them to share any concerns or incidents they encounter, and be proactive in addressing them in a supportive and non-judgmental manner. Regular check-ins can help ensure that your children feel heard, valued, and supported.

4. **Lead by Example:** Model the behaviors and values you wish to instill in your children. Demonstrate assertiveness, empathy, and healthy communication in your interactions with others, both at home and in public. Your actions speak louder than words, and your children will learn valuable lessons by observing how you navigate various situations.

5. **Reinforce Positive Behaviors:** Celebrate and reinforce moments when your children demonstrate healthy behaviors and boundaries. Offer praise and encouragement to acknowledge their efforts and reinforce the importance of standing up for themselves and others.

6. **Create a Supportive Environment:** Foster a supportive and nurturing environment where your children feel safe to express themselves and seek guidance when needed. Encourage them to ask questions, share their thoughts and feelings, and seek assistance in navigating challenging situations.

By consistently reinforcing and practicing healthy behaviors with your children, you empower them to navigate the complexities of relationships and interactions with confidence and resilience. Remember that learning is an ongoing process, and each opportunity for reinforcement and practice brings your children one step closer to developing strong, healthy boundaries and relationships. So, keep the conversations going, seize teachable moments as they arise, and continue to guide and support your children on their journey toward emotional well-being and self-empowerment.

CHAPTER 31
KEEPING KIDS SAFE

Educate and empower your children to recognize and respond to potential risks and dangers.

In the complex landscape of co-parenting with a toxic individual, ensuring the safety and well-being of your children is paramount. Toxic individuals may employ manipulation tactics that can be considered a form of grooming behavior, aimed at eroding boundaries, self-esteem, autonomy, and self-confidence in children. As a parent, it's crucial to educate your children on recognizing and responding to such tactics, as well as equipping them with the knowledge and tools to stay safe from potential harm.

Here are some strategies for keeping your kids safe in the face of toxic dynamics:

1. **Educate Your Child on "Tricky People":** Teach your child about the concept of "tricky people" who may seek to groom and harm them. Explain that these individuals may use manipulation tactics to lower or eliminate boundaries and that it's essential to recognize and respond assertively to such behavior. What's important to note here is that tricky people aren't always strangers—they can be anyone, including a parent. This type of grooming within a familial setting often involves the parent using manipulative tactics to control or alienate the child from the other

parent or family members, potentially causing emotional and psychological harm.

Here's an example:

Sharia, a 10-year-old, loved both her parents dearly. After her parents' divorce, she began spending weekends with her father, David, who seemed to change after the separation. During her visits, David would often speak negatively about her mother, subtly at first, then more openly, claiming her mother was too busy to truly love Sharia or care for her well-being.

He presented himself as the better, more loving parent by offering Sharia lavish gifts and taking her on fun outings, telling her, "These are our special secrets. Don't tell your mom; she might ruin our fun." He framed his behavior as acts of love, making her feel special and cherished in his presence.

However, David also began questioning Sharia about her life with her mother, using Sharia's answers to criticize her mother further and validating his own role in Sharia's life. "See, I'd never do that to you. We have a special bond," he'd say. Over time, Sharia started feeling confused and torn between her parents. She felt guilty enjoying time with her mom and began withdrawing, unsure whom to trust.

It wasn't until Sharia's mother noticed her growing distress and withdrawal that she initiated a conversation about Sharia's time with her father. With gentle questioning, she learned about the gifts, the outings, and the secrets. Recognizing these as classic grooming behaviors aimed at alienating her from her daughter, Sharia's mother sought professional help.

Together with a therapist, they worked through the manipulation tactics used by David, helping Sharia understand the situation without feeling caught in the middle. They established open communication and set clear, healthy boundaries to protect Sharia's emotional well-being.

This story illustrates how toxic parents can manipulate children's emotions and perceptions for their own gain, highlighting the necessity for the other parent and caregivers to teach their children to spot tricky people.

2. **Discuss Grooming Behaviors:** Have age-appropriate conversations with your child about grooming behaviors and how to identify them. Empower them to trust their instincts and speak up if they feel uncomfortable or unsafe in any situation.

    a. **Define Grooming in Simple Terms:** Begin by explaining what grooming is in a way that is suitable for your child's age and understanding. You might say, "Sometimes, people try to make friends with you or give you special attention, not because they are genuinely nice, but because they want you to do things that aren't okay. This is called grooming, and it's important to know about it so you can keep yourself safe."

    b. **Identify Behaviors:** Help your child understand the specific behaviors that could indicate grooming. Explain that these can include someone giving them gifts frequently, asking them to keep secrets from their other parent or anyone else, or showing them affection only when they agree to do what the person wants. Make it clear that a parent should not involve them in adult issues, use them as a confidant for problems with the other parent, or expect them to manage adult emotions.

    c. **Empower with Knowledge:** Teach your child that they have the right to say no, that their body and their feelings belong to them, and no one should make them feel uncomfortable. For instance, discuss the difference between good and bad secrets: good secrets can be things like surprise parties, which are revealed after a short time and make everyone happy, whereas bad secrets make them feel uneasy or scared and are never supposed to be told.

d. **Encourage Open Communication:** Create a trusting environment where your child feels safe to talk about anything that bothers them. Assure them that they won't be in trouble for speaking up about uncomfortable situations, even if it involves the other parent. Let them know it's okay to tell you if they ever feel pressured, scared, or confused by anyone's actions, including the co-parent.

e. **Practice Scenarios:** Run through hypothetical scenarios to help your child practice what to say or do if they feel they're being groomed. Role-play responses they can use, like, "I need to talk to my mom/dad about this," or, "I'm not comfortable with keeping secrets from my mom/dad."

f. **Discuss How to Seek Help:** Educate them on how to seek help if they're ever in an uncomfortable position. This can include telling a trusted teacher, calling a relative, or using a code word with you that means they need help immediately.

3. **Promote Boundaries and Autonomy:** Reinforce the importance of setting and maintaining boundaries, respecting personal space, and asserting oneself in relationships. Encourage your child to trust their instincts and seek help if they feel threatened or endangered.

a. **Explain Boundaries Clearly:** Start by explaining what boundaries are in simple, age-appropriate language. For example, you might say, "Boundaries are rules we set for ourselves that tell others how we want to be treated. Just like how we have rules in games to make sure everyone plays fair and has fun, boundaries help us feel safe and respected in our relationships."

b. **Identify Healthy vs. Unhealthy Boundaries:** Help your child understand the difference between healthy and unhealthy boundaries. For instance, a healthy boundary might be telling someone they need some alone time to read or play, whereas an unhealthy boundary might involve a parent insisting on knowing all their private thoughts or feelings, which can feel invasive.

c. **Role-play Scenarios:** Use role-playing to help your child practice setting boundaries. Create scenarios where they might need to assert themselves, such as a parent asking them to keep secrets from the other parent or to relay messages between parents, which are inappropriate responsibilities for a child. Guide them on how to respectfully but firmly say things like, "I'm not comfortable talking about that," or, "I would rather not be in the middle of this."

d. **Empower Them to Say No:** Encourage your child that it's okay to say no if something doesn't feel right, even if it involves a parent. Emphasize that their feelings are important and they have the right to protect their personal space and emotions.

e. **Encourage Autonomy in Decision Making:** Allow your child to make choices about their activities, clothes, and friends within reason. This practice not only builds their self-confidence but also reinforces their sense of autonomy, helping them feel more in control of their environment and less susceptible to manipulation.

f. **Reinforce the Importance of Seeking Help:** Teach your child that it's important to reach out for help if they ever feel unsafe or if someone repeatedly disrespects their boundaries. Identify a list of trusted adults they can turn to, such as the non-toxic parent, teachers, family members, or counselors. Put the phone numbers of safe adults into their phone so they can easily contact someone in the event of an urgent issue.

g. **Model Respectful Behavior:** Demonstrate respect for your child's boundaries in your daily interactions. Show that you honor their personal space, ask permission before entering their room, and respect their wishes when they express a need for privacy. Modeling this behavior provides a practical and positive example of how they should expect to be treated by others.

4. **Teach Online Safety:** Educate your child about the potential dangers of the internet and social media, including exposure to inappropriate content, online predators, and cyberbullying. Teach them how to navigate the online world safely and responsibly.

5. **Provide Resources and Support:** Arm yourself with books, resources, and educational materials that address topics such as personal safety, body boundaries, healthy relationships, and online safety. Engage in discussions with your child about these topics regularly to reinforce key concepts and address any questions or concerns they may have.

6. **Attend Webinars and Workshops:** Take advantage of educational opportunities such as webinars and workshops offered by experts in child safety and protection. These sessions can provide valuable insights and strategies for keeping your children safe in challenging situations.

By proactively educating and empowering your children to recognize and respond to potential risks and dangers, you can help them develop the confidence, resilience, and skills they need to navigate the world safely. Remember to approach these conversations with empathy, understanding, and patience, and to provide ongoing support and guidance as your children grow and learn. Together, we can create a safer and more secure environment for our children to thrive and flourish.

☐ Read the following books to your children:

o Super Duper Safety School

o Let's Talk About Body Boundaries, Consent and Respect

o Good Pictures Bad Pictures Jr.: A Simple Plan to Protect Young Minds

o 30 Days of Sex Talks for Ages 3-7: Empowering Your Child with Knowledge of Sexual Intimacy

☐ Attend a Birds and Bees webinar

CHAPTER 32

CHECKING IN WITH YOUR KIDS

Regular check-ins provide valuable opportunities to gauge the well-being of your family dynamics and address any concerns.

Running your family like a serious business—and meaning business about raising healthy children who can survive an unhealthy parent—means prioritizing open communication and feedback from all members, including your children. Regular check-ins provide valuable opportunities to gauge the well-being of your family dynamics and address any concerns or areas for improvement proactively.

Here are some suggestions for implementing regular check-ins with your kids:

1. **Scheduled Family Meetings:** Set aside a dedicated time each week for family meetings. Choose a consistent day and time that works for everyone, such as Sunday evenings or Saturday mornings. Use this time to discuss any issues, share updates, and plan activities for the week ahead.

2. **Morning Commutes or Snuggle Time:** Take advantage of natural opportunities for one-on-one conversations with your children, such as during morning commutes to school or during snuggle

time before bed. These moments of intimacy and connection provide an ideal setting for checking in and having meaningful discussions.

3. **Ask Open-Ended Questions:** Encourage your children to express themselves by asking open-ended questions about their experiences and feelings. For example, inquire about how they would describe your family to someone else, how their week has been, and what they believe your family is doing well and where improvements could be made.

4. **Create a Safe Space for Feedback:** Foster an environment where your children feel comfortable sharing their thoughts and opinions openly. Assure them that their feedback is valued and respected, and emphasize that your goal is to create a positive and supportive family culture.

5. **Listen Actively and Responsively:** Practice active listening during check-ins, giving your full attention to your children and validating their feelings and perspectives. Respond empathetically to their feedback and collaborate on solutions or strategies for addressing any issues or concerns that arise.

Regular check-ins with your kids not only help you stay attuned to their needs and experiences but also reinforce the importance of open communication and mutual respect within your family. By prioritizing these moments of connection and reflection, you can strengthen your family bonds and create a supportive and nurturing environment where everyone feels heard, valued, and empowered to thrive.

☐ Schedule weekly family meetings. You can have a weekly agenda that includes celebrating wins and positive events, raising problems and issues to be solved as a family, and planning and making decisions as a family.

CHAPTER 33

WHEN PROBLEMS ARISE WITH THE CO-PARENT

You can navigate challenges with the co-parent and ensure that your child's best interests are prioritized and protected.

Navigating co-parenting with a toxic individual can present numerous challenges, particularly when problems or conflicts arise concerning your children's well-being. It's essential to approach these situations with caution, empathy, and a steadfast commitment to advocating for your child's best interests.

Here are some strategies to consider when facing issues with the co-parent:

1. **Believe Your Kids:** Err on the side of believing your children when they express concerns or share experiences related to their co-parent. Toxic individuals are often adept at manipulation and deceit, and your children may be more reliable sources of truth than the co-parent.

2. **Recognize Manipulation Tactics:** Toxic individuals typically employ manipulation tactics such as lying, gaslighting, and confusion tactics like word salad or "alternative facts" to obscure the truth and maintain control. Be vigilant in recognizing these

tactics and the co-parent's attempts to deceive or manipulate. When you notice a manipulative tactic, call it what it is. Calling it what it is with your child can remove the power from the perpetrator and increase your child's power to identify manipulative tactics and guard against them.

3. **Acknowledge Emotional Immaturity:** Understand that toxic individuals exhibit emotional immaturity, resembling that of a child between the ages of 4 and 8. Your children may possess greater emotional maturity and resilience than the co-parent, which underscores the importance of advocating for them and protecting them.

4. **Advocate Despite Fear and Anxiety:** Despite the fear, nausea, anxiety, and worry that may accompany confronting the co-parent or advocating for your child, it's essential to prioritize their safety and well-being above all else. Summon the courage to speak up and take action on behalf of your child, even when you may rather run the other way and hide.

5. **Leverage Your Community of Health:** Engage your trusted network of friends, family members, therapists, and other supportive individuals in addressing issues with the co-parent. Seek their guidance, advice, and emotional support as you navigate challenging situations and advocate for your child's best interests.

6. **Reinforce Healthy Behavior:** Utilize the resources within your Community of Health to reinforce healthy behavior and underscore what is and isn't acceptable in your child's interactions with the co-parent. Provide your child with a supportive and nurturing environment where they feel empowered to assert their boundaries and advocate for themselves, and see those same behaviors modeled in the community surrounding them and

receive encouragement from their community to advocate for themselves.

By remaining vigilant, advocating for your child's well-being, and leveraging the support of your Community of Health, you can navigate challenges with the co-parent and ensure that your child's best interests are prioritized and protected.

- ☐ Only communicate with your ex via text or co-parenting app so that your conversations are documented.

- ☐ Use a co-parent communication app such as OurFamilyWizard, AppClose, 2Houses, or similar so that you only communicate with your co-parent in writing.

- ☐ Use grey rock and yellow rock statements in your communications with your co-parent.

- ☐ Use AI tools such as ChatGPT or Gemini to assist you in writing unemotional messages to your co-parent.

- ☐ If you must speak with your co-parent in person, have a security camera installed outside or inside your home so that the conversation is recorded.

- ☐ Should you need to speak with your co-parent in person, have a supportive and reasonable friend present or on the phone with you for moral support. The friend shouldn't involve themselves in the conversation unless your co-parent's behavior rises to the level of offensive, threatening, or violent.

- ☐ Document troubling incidents in a physical notebook or virtual notebook such as Google Docs, Evernote, OneNote, or similar. Your documentation should include the date and time of the incident, all details of the incident as reported by your child, and any screenshots of texts or messages with your co-parent about the incident.

CHAPTER 34
CALLING IN THE CAVALRY

While this book provides valuable insights and strategies for navigating co-parenting with a toxic individual, there may be situations where the behavior of the other parent crosses a line and poses a serious threat to your child's safety and well-being. In these cases, it's essential to call in the cavalry—to enlist the support and intervention of trusted professionals and resources who can help protect your child and address the situation effectively.

Here are some key resources and individuals to consider reaching out to in times of crisis:

1. **Pediatrician:** Your child's pediatrician can serve as a trusted ally and resource in situations where your child's safety or well-being is at risk. They can provide guidance, support, and referrals to appropriate services or specialists as needed, including calling in Child Protective Services if necessary.

2. **Child Therapist or Brightline:** Brightline is an invaluable resource for families facing challenges related to mental health, behavior, and well-being. Their team of experts can offer personalized

support, therapy, and resources to help address complex issues and ensure the safety of your child. If your child has an established relationship with a therapist, you can reach out to them for guidance, assistance, and referrals to appropriate services. Therapists are mandated reporters who may report serious situations to your local Child Protective Services office.

3. **School Counselors:** School counselors play a crucial role in supporting students' social, emotional, and academic needs. Reach out to your child's school counselor if you have concerns about your child's well-being or if you need assistance navigating difficult situations involving the other parent.

4. **Parent Coordinator or Parent Coach:** A parent coordinator is an individual who can work with one or both parents to provide parenting guidance and to mediate problems between parents. It may be possible to get a parent coordinator assigned to your family via a court order, or via an agreement with your co-parent in mediation. Alternatively, you could work with a parent coach who can help you navigate specific parenting issues or give you overall parenting guidance. Working with a parent coach can help you feel less alone and more supported. In some cases, parent coaches are mandated reporters who can determine whether an issue your family is facing requires intervention by your local Child Protective Services office.

5. **Attorney:** If the behavior of the other parent poses a significant threat to your child's safety or violates the terms of your parenting plan, consult with your attorney to explore legal options. They can advise you on steps such as modifying the parenting plan, seeking supervised visits, or obtaining a restraining order to protect your child from harm.

6. **Healthy Friends and Family:** Lean on your support network of healthy friends and family members who can provide emotional

support, assistance, and practical help in times of crisis. They can serve as emergency contacts and provide a safe haven for you and your child if needed.

7. **Law Enforcement:** In situations of immediate danger or physical abuse, do not hesitate to contact law enforcement for assistance. Your child's safety is paramount, and law enforcement can intervene to ensure their protection and well-being. Consider seeking a restraining order against the other parent if necessary to prevent further harm.

Remember, you are your child's greatest ally and advocate. While dealing with the tantrums and manipulative tactics of the other parent may be challenging, your priority is to ensure the safety and well-being of your child. If you ever feel that your life or your child's life is in danger, do not hesitate to seek help from trusted professionals and authorities. Always work to protect our children and create a safe and nurturing environment for them to thrive.

Important Note About CPS

It's crucial to exercise caution when considering contacting Child Protective Services (CPS) regarding your co-parent, as doing so could be perceived by family courts as manipulative or retaliatory. No one wants CPS involved in their family life, and if your child genuinely requires assistance, it's far more effective for a mandated reporter—like a doctor or therapist—to reach out to CPS rather than you taking that step yourself. When you initiate contact, it can be misconstrued as an attempt at parental alienation, a concept that, while often criticized as junk science, still holds weight in some courtrooms. Therefore, it's essential to tread carefully—seeking support from healthcare professionals allows them to assess the situation and determine if further intervention is warranted, thereby protecting your credibility and prioritizing your child's well-being.

CHAPTER 35

CONTROL ONLY WHAT YOU CAN CONTROL

Grant me the serenity to accept the things I cannot change, the courage to change the things I can, and the wisdom to know the difference.

As a parent navigating the complex dynamics of co-parenting with a narcissistic or toxic ex, you must focus only on what you can control—specifically, the environment in your own home. The atmosphere you create for your children is vital in helping them develop resilience and strength to withstand the challenges they face, particularly when dealing with the delusional narratives of a toxic co-parent. Your home should be a sanctuary—a safe place where your children feel loved, valued, and empowered to believe their own minds.

Controlling Your Home Environment

The reality is that there will be unsavory situations and behaviors in the other parent's home that you cannot control. Whether it's emotional manipulation, gaslighting, or unhealthy dynamics, those experiences are outside your influence. However, what you can control is the environment your children return to after their time with the other parent. This is where you can set the tone, build a foundation of trust, and instill the values that will help them navigate the complexities of life.

Create a space where your children feel safe to express themselves, share their feelings, and grow emotionally. This means making your home a refuge from the chaos they may encounter elsewhere. Fill it with love, laughter, and open communication. Establish routines that foster security and predictability, allowing your children to feel grounded and confident.

Avoiding the Trap of Micromanagement

As a caring and protective parent, it's natural to want to shield your children from negative influences, but it's crucial to avoid micromanaging their experiences, especially regarding the other parent's home. Doing so can create tension and may lead to your children feeling caught in the middle of a conflict that isn't theirs to resolve.

Using self-care tools and self-control is essential in this regard. Recognize that you cannot dictate the environment of the other parent's home, nor should you try. Instead, focus on maintaining a healthy perspective. Allow your children to have their own experiences, even if they include unsavory elements. This not only fosters their independence but also teaches them how to navigate complexities outside your control.

The Risks of Being Seen as Controlling

It's important to understand that if you attempt to control too much—especially the dynamics in the other parent's household—you run the risk of being labeled as a controlling or uncooperative parent. This perception can lead to increased conflict and pushback, which is the last thing you want for your children. Instead of fostering a sense of security, micromanagement can make them feel like they're being scrutinized or pressured to choose sides. Worse yet, your co-parent could leverage their skills of persuasion, projection, and confusion and raise issues with your behavior with your children's therapists, their teachers, and in family court, potentially painting *you* as the unsafe parent. Of course, this is counter to your goals and doesn't help your children in any way.

For instance, if your co-parent is letting your children watch too much television or play with their devices for longer than you would at your home, this is probably not a battle worth fighting. However, if your co-parent is exposing your children to adult entertainment, drugs, alcohol, or violence, this would likely be worth bringing up to your support network to get guidance and assistance on how to address these more serious issues.

Unsafe behavior aside, even though you know well that their co-parent is unhealthy, dysfunctional, and possibly unsafe for your children to be around, when you allow your children to develop their own relationships, even with their toxic parent, you show them that they can navigate their own feelings and learn valuable lessons about relationships. They will understand that while some behaviors may be problematic, they have the agency to respond in ways that protect their well-being. And that's what all of this is about—teaching them how not to fall for the toxic traps their other parent, and perhaps other people in their lives, will set for them.

Maintaining Your Focus

At the end of the day, your focus should be on creating a nurturing environment where your children can flourish. Encourage them to embrace their own identities, independent of the toxic dynamics they may face elsewhere. Help them build the mental and emotional tools necessary to recognize unhealthy behaviors and trust their instincts.

By embracing what you can control—your home environment and the values you instill in your children—you empower them to navigate their own lives with strength and resilience. It's a journey that requires patience and love, but by focusing on your home as a safe haven, you lay the groundwork for your children to grow into confident individuals who believe their own minds, regardless of the challenges they encounter with a toxic co-parent.

In the end, remember that you are not just shaping their childhood—you are preparing them for adulthood. By fostering a positive, stable, and loving environment, you give them the best possible chance to thrive, no matter what they face outside your home.

CHAPTER 36

GIVING YOURSELF GRACE ON THE CO-PARENTING JOURNEY

*Your strength lies not in being perfect
but in your determination to keep moving forward.*

When co-parenting with a narcissist, the path is often anything but straightforward. It's easy to feel like every decision, every interaction, and every boundary you set must be perfect—especially when you're doing everything you can to protect your children and yourself from manipulation. But here's the truth: you're human. You're going to make mistakes. And that's okay.

Co-parenting with a narcissist is one of the most emotionally taxing experiences anyone can go through. It's an uphill battle that often feels relentless. Even with all the tools you've learned, even with boundaries in place, there will be moments when you feel like you've failed. Maybe you reacted to a provocation from your ex, or perhaps you felt worn down and let a boundary slip. In these moments, it's essential to remember that grace is just as important as resilience.

Mistakes Will Happen—And That's Okay

Parenting in any situation is challenging, and when you add a toxic co-parent into the mix, it amplifies the difficulty. One of the most important things you can do for yourself is to accept that mistakes are part of the process. You might find yourself reacting emotionally, or giving in to an argument, or second-guessing yourself. It's natural. It happens.

You're bound to have days when you feel tired, vulnerable, or defeated. Days when the stress of constant conflict or manipulation weighs heavily on you. On those days, remind yourself that you're doing your best. You're learning, adapting, and navigating a situation that very few people truly understand unless they've been through it.

Forgive yourself for the occasional slip-up. It's not about being perfect, but about showing up for your children and yourself consistently—even when it's hard. Grace doesn't mean lowering your standards or giving in to the toxicity. It means accepting your humanity and being kind to yourself in the moments where you feel like you're not enough.

Keep Using the Tools You've Learned

Every tool you've learned in this journey—whether it's setting boundaries, using structured communication, or practicing emotional regulation—is there to help guide you. But just like any new skill, it takes time and practice to fully integrate them into your life. You won't always get it right the first time, or even the second or third.

Remember, the key is consistency, not perfection. When you slip, it's not the end of the road. Instead of focusing on the mistake, focus on how you can apply the tools you've learned next time. Use every setback as a learning experience. Over time, these tools will become second nature, and you'll find yourself better equipped to handle the challenges that come your way.

If you find that your boundaries wavered or you reacted in a way you wish you hadn't, take a deep breath. Reflect on what happened, adjust your approach, and commit to using the tools again. The strength is in returning to those tools time and time again.

Boundaries Are Your Superpower

It's easy to feel guilty when you enforce a boundary with a narcissistic co-parent. They often push back, manipulate, or even attempt to guilt-trip you into feeling like you're the unreasonable one. But boundaries are not just necessary—they are essential. They are your power in a situation where control often feels out of reach.

If a boundary slips, or you find yourself feeling overwhelmed by your ex's constant boundary-pushing, take it as a moment to regroup. Remind yourself why those boundaries are there in the first place: to protect your peace, your well-being, and your children. Boundaries are not walls of isolation—they are lines of protection. The occasional slip doesn't mean the boundary is broken forever. You can reset it, reinforce it, and stand strong again.

Each time you re-establish your boundaries, you are reinforcing the message that you will not be controlled by manipulation. This is a powerful stance for you and an important lesson for your children, who will learn from your example. The strength you show in maintaining these boundaries, even after they've been tested, is a testament to your resilience.

Strength Comes in Staying the Course

Co-parenting with a narcissist is not a short sprint—it's a long, often exhausting marathon. Strength doesn't mean never faltering, it means staying the course despite the challenges. It means showing up, day after day, for yourself and your children, even when the road seems never-ending.

You've already shown incredible strength by choosing to protect your children and yourself from a toxic co-parent. You've learned tools, set boundaries, and developed strategies that many never have to face. But strength also lies in the moments of vulnerability—in the moments where you admit that this is hard and allow yourself to rest, regroup, and try again.

When you stumble or feel like you've failed, remind yourself that strength is in the persistence, not the perfection. Each time you get up and face another day, another challenge, another interaction, you are proving your strength. You're proving that no matter how difficult co-parenting with a narcissist is, you're committed to doing what's best for your children.

Keep Moving Forward

In the end, your journey is not defined by a single mistake, a tough day, or a challenging moment. It's defined by the fact that you keep moving forward, one step at a time. You are learning, growing, and adapting in an incredibly difficult situation.

Giving yourself grace doesn't mean lowering your standards or letting go of the tools you've worked so hard to learn. It means recognizing that you are human and that this journey is full of ups and downs. You will falter, and that's okay. What matters is that you keep putting one foot in front of the other. You keep putting the tools into practice, reinforcing your boundaries, and showing your children what resilience looks like.

Your strength lies not in being perfect but in your determination to keep moving forward, no matter how difficult the road may be.

CONCLUSION

We've explored a multitude of strategies, insights, and resources aimed at empowering you to navigate this challenging terrain while prioritizing the well-being and safety of your child. From setting firm boundaries to reinforcing healthy values, from advocating for your child to calling in the cavalry when needed, this book has provided a comprehensive guide to help you weather the storms and navigate the complexities of co-parenting with grace and resilience.

Throughout these pages, we've emphasized the importance of maintaining a legacy of wellness for your child—a legacy built on a foundation of love, empathy, and unyielding commitment to their growth and happiness. While the road may be fraught with obstacles and challenges, remember that you are not alone in this journey. You have a community of support, resources, and guidance to lean on, and together, we can overcome any adversity that comes our way.

As you continue your co-parenting journey, remember to trust your instincts, advocate fiercely for your child, and prioritize their safety and well-being above all else. Cherish the moments of connection and joy, celebrate the victories, no matter how small, and persevere through the trials with strength and resilience.

Above all, remember that you are your child's greatest ally and role model. Your love, support, and continued dedication are the greatest gifts you can give them as they navigate the complexities of life. And as you embark on this journey, know that you are laying the groundwork for a future filled with love, resilience, and boundless possibilities for your child and generations to come.

Thank you for entrusting me with a part of your journey, and may your path be filled with love, light, and endless blessings as you continue to guide and nurture your child through the highs and lows of life.

I'll leave you with the same guidance I give my own children when they must navigate the erratic, volatile journey with their co-parent who consistently works to replace their reality with his own confusing and convoluted version:

Believe your own mind.

With heartfelt gratitude and best wishes,

Ayo Bomani

Some parting thoughts:

- Please tell us how this book has positively impacted you by leaving an Amazon review.

- We'd love to be part of your support community and follow your journey—join the Believe Your Own Mind community and tell us how you're doing.

- Let the Believe Your Own Mind app be your daily cheerleader— add the Believe Your Own Mind app to your network of support.

AFTERWORD

I finished writing this book and realized I had one more key point to share.

You may have gotten into a romantic relationship with your co-parent because your naturally empathetic nature led you to look past any red flags and see the good in them. Even now, when tensions run high, you may still be able to understand how your co-parent reaches certain conclusions, even if the thoughts that informed their conclusions are disordered, Machiavellian, and fall well outside the boundaries of objective reality. You might find yourself thinking about the many reasons behind their actions—their past experiences, their emotional wounds. It's okay to have some level of understanding and compassion for your co-parent—you are a human being experiencing the wide range of human emotions and some of those emotions might include feeling sad or sorry for your co-parent even when they are in the wrong.

I could say a lot here about having misplaced hope that a leopard will change its spots, about codependency, and even about Stockholm syndrome, but I'm not a therapist. Instead, I'll offer this:

You might understand why an unsound high-rise collapsed with occupants inside or why a tornado tore through a small town, devastating everything in its path. That understanding does not negate the reality of the destruction and loss; *it simply provides context*.

But understanding the "why" doesn't stop you from getting down to the real work of rendering aid to those in need. Especially in the moments when you or your child are nursing the wounds and PTSD caused by your co-parent, and your co-parent responds to the consequences of their actions by figuratively or literally falling to their knees before you, arms outstretched to the sky as if begging for mercy, and bellowing unironically, "Why are you doing this to me?! What have I done to deserve this?!", remember that although you can understand the nature of a natural disaster, you must focus your energy where it is needed most—rendering aid to those who are in harm's way.

You've got this.

Believe your own mind. Always.

www.ingramcontent.com/pod-product-compliance
Lightning Source LLC
LaVergne TN
LVHW020948200726
843508LV00004B/1392